GOD IS

A WORKBOOK OF THE DOCTRINE OF GOD

Grace Publications Trust

Published by
GRACE PUBLICATIONS TRUST
139 Grosvenor Avenue,
London, N5 2NH

First published 1985

ISBN 0 9 46462 06 2

Distributed by
EVANGELICAL PRESS
16/18 High Street, Welwyn,
Herts, AL6 9EQ,
England

Typeset by Inset Typesetters, Chappel, Essex
Printed in Great Britain by Heffers Printers Limited, Cambridge

PREFACE

The source material for this course of study was originally prepared by Richard Chester, B.D. of Abbey Baptist Church, Abingdon, and arranged in this workbook form by Grace Baptist Mission for translation into Tamil and use among the Tamil Baptist congregations of South India.

Requests to use this course of study have been received from other parts of the world. It has, therefore, been thoroughly revised and is now published in English. This is the second workbook. The first – God Speaks, a Workbook of the Bible – was published in 1980.

It is suggested that this material can be used in a variety of ways:

1. As a correspondence course, with the test papers on each lesson being sent for marking to the centre responsible for distributing the course.

2. As a workbook, for use in weekly meetings of Bible classes, or senior Sunday School classes, under the guidance of a class leader, with or without the test papers.

3. As a study course for house meetings or study groups, Christian Unions, etc.

4. As material for discussion groups, after-church fellowships, or youth groups.

5. As follow-up material for teaching new converts.

6. As lesson material for camps, summer schools and classes, designed to provide instruction for Christian workers.

There is much value in the student writing out the various scripture verses as indicated in the lessons:

1. So that all relevant material is available in the one book at the conclusion of the study,

2. So that it is demonstrated that what the lessons teach is always drawn from the Bible, and

3. So that one or two key Bible passages, being used more than once, are fixed firmly in the student's thinking, by being written in several lessons.

It is anticipated that permission to translate this material into other languages will be sought from the publishers: Grace Publications Trust.

CONTENTS

THE DOCTRINE OF GOD

SUBJECT: KNOWING GOD *Part 1*

COURSE 2
Lesson No. 1

SUBJECT: KNOWING GOD – part 1

COURSE NO. 2
Lesson No. 1

Write out:

John 17:3

. . . .

. . . .

. . . .

To think about:

". . . man never attains to a true self-knowledge, until he has previously contemplated the face of God . . ."
from "Institutes of the Christian Religion" – Book 1, ch. 1 (John Calvin, 1509–64)

"Man's chief and highest end is to glorify God and fully to enjoy him for ever . . ."
from *Larger Westminster Catechism,* 1648.

1. INTRODUCTION

The purpose of this course of studies is that we might know God.

A. We need to know God because:

☐ He is our Maker and therefore has the right to expect us to know him.

☐ He intended that we should know him; therefore we offend him when we fail to know him.

☐ We shall not ourselves be satisfied while we fail to be what we were made to be – knowers of God.

☐ After death we must meet him and give an account of our behaviour in this life.

Look up these verses and put the correct number in the box to which the references relate.

1	2	3	4
Acts 17:31 Hebrews 9:27	Psalm 100:3 Romans 11:36	Ecclesiastes 6:12 Ephesians 2:12	Deuteronomy 28:15 Romans 8:7, 8

LET US NOW SEEK TO KNOW GOD. There is no better thing that we can do!

Check, then proceed The correct answers on page 1 are, from top to bottom: 2 : 4 : 3 : 1

To think about:

"... such ... knowledge expresses the apprehension of the truth by the whole nature of man. It is not an acquaintance with facts as external, nor an intellectual conviction of their reality, but an appropriation of them ... as an influencing power into the very being of him who knows them".
from commentary on John 17:3 by Dr. B. F. Westcott, 1881.

Introduction, continued

B. Knowing a person is *quite different* from knowing a subject like mathematics or history.

Knowing a person is *quite different* from knowing facts about a person.

The facts of a subject are lifeless things. You can know them. *They do not know you.* There is no experience of living contact between you and them.

A person is a living being. Knowing a person means to have some real contact with him, so *he knows you also.* There is an experience of living contact between you and him.

SO *knowing God* is quite different from knowing *facts about God.*

Write out:

Job 42:5

. . . .

. . . .

. . . .

IN THIS LESSON we answer the question: *Is there a God for us to know?*

2. EVIDENCES THAT GOD EXISTS

A. The Bible nowhere argues a detailed proof for the existence of God. It always *assumes* that God is. The Bible states the fact without giving proof.

Read:

Acts 17:24

Write out:

Genesis 1:1

. . . .

. . . .

B. So the existence of God is a fact we must accept BY FAITH.

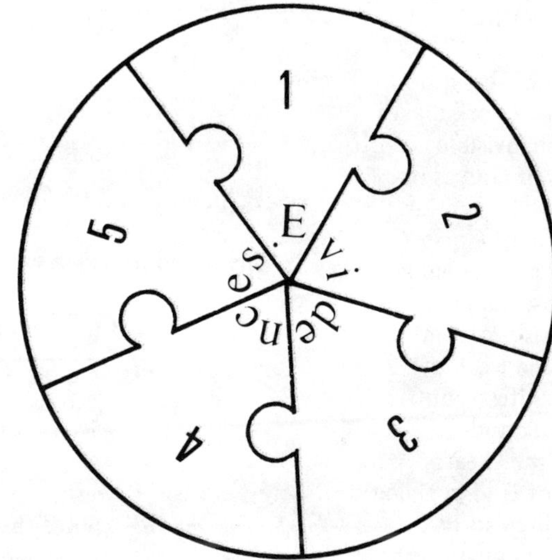

Cross out the wrong words

"anyone who comes to God must	* pretend * hope * prove * believe	that he exists

and that he rewards those who earnestly seek him."

General Revelation
See – Course 1 lesson 1 page 3

C. To accept the existence of God by faith *is not unreasonable.* There are at least *five* evidences which make it very reasonable to believe that God is. Most of these evidences arise from the General Revelation of God in the natural world and in people, but they are referred to in the Bible.

WE SHALL NOW LOOK AT THESE FIVE EVIDENCES.

Check, then proceed: Turn to Hebrews 11:6 and make sure you have crossed out the incorrect words on page 3

Evidence 1

Write out:

Romans 1:19, 20

. . . .

. . . .

. . . .

. . . .

. . . .

. . . .

. . . .

To think about:

". . . the visible creation as God's handiwork makes manifest the invisible perfections of God as its Creator . . . thus, a clear apprehension of God's perfections may be gained from his observable handiwork . . . it is not a finite cause that the work of creation manifests, but eternal power and divinity of the Creator . . . the design of God in giving so open a disclosure . . . is that all men might be without excuse".

from a commentary on Romans 1:20 by Prof. John Murray, 1960.

The world in which we live has come into being either:

BY CHANCE — or — BY A CREATOR

There is no other possibility.

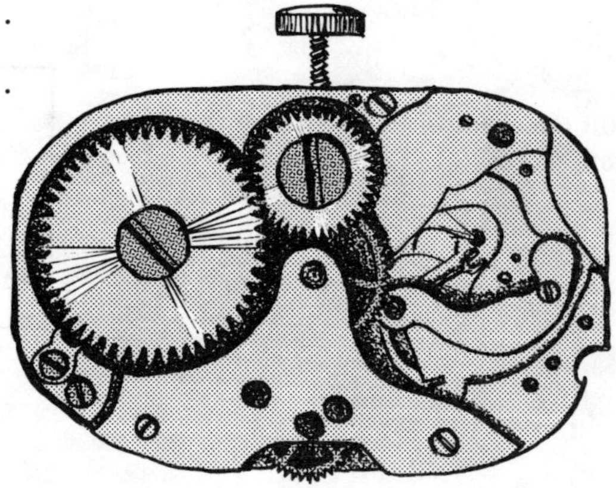

Since there are so many signs of careful DESIGN and PURPOSE in every part of nature, it is utterly illogical to believe that it has all come by chance. DESIGN and PURPOSE can only be the work of a wise and powerful person. This is what Paul argues in the scripture you have written out above.

HERE IS EVIDENCE 1 ▷ DESIGN IN CREATION PRESUPPOSES A CREATOR

Evidence 2

Write out:

Acts 17:29

. . . .

. . . .

. . . .

. . . .

Read:

Psalm 94:9

To think about:

"Man himself is far more excellent than an image of wood and stone; how much more excellent still must be the great fountain and source of all *our* wisdom and intelligence."
from commentary on Acts 17:29 by Albert Barnes (1798–1870).

Adam was made either:

BY A PERSONAL CREATOR — or — BY A NON-PERSONAL CAUSE

There is no other possibility.

Since the world is full of personal beings, it is utterly illogical to believe they have all come from a non-personal cause. A river cannot rise higher than its source; the personal cannot come from the impersonal.

And where do we get our ideas of truth, beauty, goodness, freedom and love from? If the world came from a non-personal cause, how have these moral values arisen? This is what Paul argues in the scripture you have written out above.

PERSONALITY belongs only to those who can appreciate moral values.

HERE IS EVIDENCE 2

▷ HUMAN PERSONALITY PRESUPPOSES A PERSONAL GOD

Evidence 3

Write out:

Romans 2:14–15

. . . .

. . . .

. . . .

. . . .

. . . .

. . . .

. . . .

. . . .

. . . .

. . . .

To think about:

"The moral history of mankind shows that every great reform has been brought about by individuals who stood out against the whole age in which they lived . . . and at times risked their lives in obedience to the truth as they saw it . . . In his conscience man is confronted by a super-human, a divine will . . . his experiences with this will are such that he feels absolutely . . . bound to submit to it".

from *The Conscience* by O. Hallesby (1879–1961).

Sometimes we feel:

WE OUGHT — or — WE OUGHT NOT

to do certain things. This inner compulsion about what is right and what is wrong is not because we will be paid for doing these things or because everyone else does them. Conscience is not merely a reflection of public opinion, because sometimes good changes in moral behaviour are opposed by public opinion.

If this world has come by chance and has no personal creator, where has this sense of right and wrong come from? It is utterly illogical to believe it has come from a non-personal source. This is what Paul argues in the scripture you have written out above.

HERE IS EVIDENCE 3 ▷ HUMAN CONSCIENCE PRESUPPOSES A MORAL GOD

Write out:

Acts 17:23

. . . .

. . . .

. . . .

. . . .

. . . .

To think about:

". . . when you see the swallows flying to a place, though you never saw the place, yet you must needs gather that there is one . . . so, when you see in every man's soul an instigation (instinct) to seek God though men never saw him . . . yet this argues that there is a deity which they intend (seek)".

from an essay on *Natural Theology* by John Preston (Puritan preacher) 1587–1628.

Everywhere in the world one finds that people worship some god. There is an instinct to worship in everyone. Even in godless cultures peoples' instinct to worship is not destroyed but is directed to some leading man instead of to God.

People everywhere have this capacity to worship, even though it may be ignorantly and crudely used. It is utterly illogical to think that such a capacity would arise if there were no Supreme Being. Where could the idea of worship of a higher being have come from, if man has developed from a lower lifeless cause? The idea of worship can only have been put into our nature by the God who made us.

HERE IS EVIDENCE 4

▷ THE HUMAN ABILITY TO WORSHIP PRESUPPOSES THAT GOD EXISTS

The four evidences we have so far looked at which make it reasonable to believe that God exists, come from the world in which we live and from our own human nature. They are:

Evidence 1	FROM NATURAL WORLD	Design in creation	A CREATOR
Evidence 2	FROM HUMAN NATURE	Human personality	A PERSONAL GOD
Evidence 3		Human conscience	A MORAL GOD
Evidence 4		Ability to worship	THAT GOD IS

There is one more evidence that God exists which we will notice.

Evidence 5

Write out:

John 1:18

....

....

....

....

Read:

John 14:6–9

Jesus Christ claimed that he showed what God is like. Jesus was either deceitful or mad or he was truthful when he said this. The rest of his life and teaching was *not* that of a deceitful or mad man. Therefore his claim must be true; he revealed the God who is.

This evidence is what is called God's Special Revelation of himself.

SPECIAL REVELATION
See – Course 1
lesson 1
page 6

HERE IS EVIDENCE **5** ▷ JESUS CHRIST REVEALED THE GOD WHO IS

3. APPLICATION

The five evidences we have now looked at are surely enough to show that it is reasonable to believe God exists and that he is a personal creator.

Why then do not all people believe in the true God?

Write out:

Psalm 10:4

. . . .

. . . .

. . . .

To think about:

". . . heathenism is not the primeval religion, from which man might gradually have risen to the knowledge of the true God, but is, on the contrary, the result of a falling away from the known original revelation of the true God in his works".
quoted in a commentary on Romans 1:21 by Prof. John Murray (1898–1975)

So if people do not believe in God,

is it because	1	they do not want to believe?
or because	2	there is no evidence of him?
or because	3	they do not need to believe?

Which is correct? 1, 2, or 3?

FILL IN THE CORRECT ANSWER HERE ☐

Write out:

Psalm 14:1

. . . .

. . . .

. . . .

Check, then proceed: The correct answer on page 9 is : 1

THE CONCLUSION OF THIS LESSON IS:

To believe that God exists and that we can know him is not unreasonable.

There are at least five evidences that belief in God is reasonable.

To think about:

"He who often thinks of God, will have a larger mind than the man who simply plods around this narrow globe . . . The most excellent study for expanding the soul, is the science of Christ, and him crucified, and the knowledge of the Godhead in the glorious Trinity. Nothing will so enlarge the intellect, nothing so magnify the whole soul of man, as a devout, earnest, continued investigation of the great subject of the Deity.

. . . I know nothing which can so comfort the soul; so calm the swelling billows of sorrow and grief; so speak peace to the winds of trial, as a devout musing upon the subject of the Godhead".

(C. H. Spurgeon, 1834–1892)

My name is .... My address is ....

QUESTIONS ABOUT LESSON 1

Only one answer is correct. Put here the number of the correct answer.

A. The knowledge of God is something that

1. Everyone needs to have
2. Humans cannot have
3. Could be useful to some people

☐

B. Knowing a person should mean

1. Just learning all you can about them
2. Meeting them and having contact with them
3. Listening to what others say about them

☐

C. It is most likely that things which show clever design

1. Have been carefully designed by someone
2. Design themselves
3. Happen by chance

☐

D. Since we have human personality, it is most likely that

1. We came into being by chance
2. Some impersonal force caused us
3. Our maker is a person also

☐

E. Since all people have some idea of worship, it is most likely that

1. There is a Supreme Being higher than us
2. They get the idea from ministers
3. Our parents put the idea into us

☐

F. A knowledge of God is something which

1. Slowly develops from the wisdom of our ancestors
2. Can only be known in certain parts of the world
3. People everywhere could have, if they wished

☐

Now send your answers to: ....

They will be marked and returned to you in due course

THE DOCTRINE OF GOD

SUBJECT: KNOWING GOD *Part 2*

COURSE 2
Lesson No. 2

SUBJECT: KNOWING GOD – part 2

COURSE NO. 2
Lesson No. 2

In lesson one we saw:

five evidences that make belief in God to be reasonable and that knowing a *person* is different from knowing *facts about a person.*

But these five evidences are merely *facts about God*!

To think about:

". . . Of ourselves we are as ignorant with respect to the nature of God as is the beetle with respect to the nature of man . . ."
Ulrich Zwingli (Swiss Reformer) 1484–1531.

In this lesson we shall see:

how God may be known *personally*.

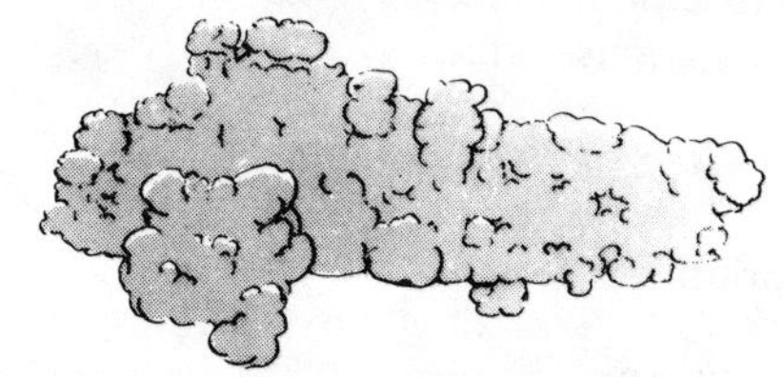

1. INTRODUCTION – a problem!

People can know other people whose natures are similar to their own. But how can people know God whose divine nature is so different from their human nature?

Write out:

Isaiah 40:18

. . . .

. . . .

. . . .

There are three things about human nature which make people very different from God and so prevent them knowing God. These three things are:

2. THREE DIFFERENCES BETWEEN PEOPLE AND GOD

A. *The first difference*

People are physical creatures. This means:

(i) THEY ARE LIMITED BY THEIR BODIES

They can only be in one place at one time

(ii) THEY ARE LIMITED IN TIME

Their lives are measured in days and minutes

(iii) THEY ARE LIMITED BY IGNORANCE

They can only know what is slowly learnt

Look up these verses:

Put a number in the box to which that verse refers.

1. Job 11:7–8
2. II Corinthians 5:1–6
3. Psalm 90:10

BODY	
TIME	
IGNORANCE	

Now write out:

John 4:24
(first part only)

....

This tells us that God is a *spirit* Being. Therefore he is not limited by any of the things that limit people.

 CREATURELINESS MAKES PEOPLE DIFFERENT FROM GOD

Creatureliness means that people's bodies are made of physical material and that people live in a material world.

Check, then proceed:

The correct answers on page 2 are:

2: BODY
3: TIME
1: IGNORANCE

B. *The second difference*

People are sinful creatures. This means:

(i) THEY ARE SPIRITUALLY BLIND

Sin makes them unable to understand spiritual things

(ii) THEY ARE AT ENMITY AGAINST GOD

Sin makes them hate spiritual things

(iii) THEY ARE LOST

Sin makes them go away from God

Look up these verses:

Put a number in the box to which that verse refers.

1. Ephesians 4:18
2. Romans 1:18–32
3. Romans 8:7

BLINDNESS	
ENMITY	
LOSTNESS	

To think about:

". . . Man cannot find God for the same reason as the thief cannot find the policeman . . ."

 SINFULNESS MAKES PEOPLE DIFFERENT FROM GOD

Check, then proceed: The correct answers on page 3 are:

1: BLINDNESS
3: ENMITY
2: LOSTNESS

C. *The third difference*

Even when people become Christian believers, they are like babies. This means:

(i) THEY ARE LIMITED BY INEXPERIENCE

They have to learn what life is like

(ii) THEY ARE LIMITED BY UNFAMILIARITY

They have to learn what their parents are like

(iii) THEY ARE LIMITED BY INFANT SIMPLICITY

They have to learn how to think and reason

So the unbeliever is not the only person to have difficulty in knowing God. Believers begin like babies and have to grow in knowledge.

Look up:

I Peter 2:2

Write out:

Psalm 40:5

. . . .

. . . .

. . . .

. . . .

. . . .

. . . .

This tells us that God has immense knowledge and experience. He does not need to learn anything.

IMMATURITY MAKES EVEN BELIEVERS DIFFERENT FROM GOD

Because we are so different from God, a great gulf exists between us and him.

3. GOD SOLVES THE PROBLEM

O V E R C O M E

GOD MUST our creatureliness / our sinfulness / our immaturity if we are ever to know him.

Creatureliness — page 2
Sinfulness — page 3
Immaturity — page 4

God HAS revealed himself in ways we can understand. Let us now see how.

See Course no. 1
lesson no. 1

A. *God has overcome our creatureliness* by revealing himself to us in two physical ways.

Write out:

II Peter 1:21
(last half)

. . . .

. . . .

(i) Though he is spirit, God speaks in the Bible in our human language.

Write out:

John 1:14

. . . .

. . . .

. . . .

. . . .

(ii) Though he is divine, God became human in the person of Jesus Christ.

Therefore people can know God by reading his words (the Bible) and learning from the life and teachings of Jesus Christ.

B. *God can overcome our sinfulness* by doing three things.

Write out:

Jeremiah 31:34
(last sentence only)

(i) He forgives the sins that separate a person from God.
(He can do this because Christ has died to atone for these sins)

Write out:

Ezekiel 36:26

(ii) God takes away the sinful enmity that controlled that person.

Write out:

Ezekiel 36:27

(iii) God gives his Spirit to that person, who will then know and love to obey God's will.

These three Old Testament prophecies describe what God does in these New Testament days to make people into believers. Therefore believers can know God because God's Spirit in them makes them capable of knowing him.

Summarise in your own words:

I Corinthians 2:9–12

Meditation — "is to be understood as a diligent reading of scripture and serious consideration of it; and of the employment of the thoughts, and of deep study . . . in order to find out . . . the meaning of it".
from commentary on Ps. 1:2 by Dr. John Gill (1697–1771)

Write out:

Psalm 1:2

Application:
see Course no. 1, lesson no. 10, "Doing only what God says!"

Write out:

Psalm 119:112

Write out:

II Timothy 1:12

"Believed" here means not merely the act of believing Jesus as Saviour but an attitude of depending on God throughout the whole of life.

C. *God overcomes our immaturity* by allowing us to grow up in our new relationship with him. Since God has put his Spirit into all believers, they can now grow in understanding of him, in familiarity with him and in experience of his ways by:

(i) *Meditation:* (A serious prolonged contemplation in order to understand and feel the power of a passage of scripture)

. . . .

. . . .

. . . .

(ii) *Application:* (Putting into use in daily life what we learn by meditation)

. . . .

. . . .

(iii) *Faith:* (An attitude of trusting in the goodness of God in all the circumstances of this life)

. . . .

. . . .

. . . .

. . . .

. . . .

As believers practise these three spiritual abilities, their knowledge *about God* will change into experiences of being related to God *as a person*; so they can grow up as developing children of God becoming more and more familiar with God.

4. KNOWING GOD PERSONALLY REQUIRES:

Write out:

Proverbs 1:7
(first part only)

(a) ....

....

Write out:

Psalm 34:18

(b) ....

....

....

Write out:

John 14:23

(c) ....

....

....

....

....

....

Write out:

Ephesians 3:19

(d) ....

....

....

....

....

Write one of these in the box against the verse which refers to that subject:

HUMILITY GODLY FEAR LOVE OBEDIENCE

Check, then proceed: From top to bottom, the words on page 8 should read: GODLY FEAR
HUMILITY
OBEDIENCE
LOVE

---

5. THREE THINGS WHICH, IF SEEN IN OUR LIVES, SHOW THAT WE DO KNOW GOD

Write out:

Romans 11:33

(a) ....

....

....

....

....

Write out:

Daniel 11:32
(second part only)

(b) ....

....

....

....

Write out:

Hebrews 13:5

(c) ....

....

....

....

....

....

Write one of these words in the box against the verse which refers to that subject:

COURAGE WORSHIP CONTENTMENT

Check, then proceed: From top to bottom, the words on page 9 should read: WORSHIP COURAGE CONTENTMENT

CONCLUSION OF THIS LESSON

God *may* be known personally by us

(a) because of what he has done to make himself known and

(b) by what believers may do now to learn to know him more and more.

To think about:

Check pages 8 and 9 again, and then ask yourself . . .

DO I REALLY KNOW GOD ?

My name is .... My address is ....

QUESTIONS ABOUT LESSON 2

Only one answer is correct. Put here the number of the correct answer.

A. Knowing God is naturally impossible for us because

1. God is so different from us sinful humans
2. God does not want us to know him anyway
3. God amuses himself by teasing us and deceiving us

☐

B. We can know God only if

1. We read the Bible right through once a year
2. We fast regularly and give to charity
3. He overcomes our limitations and relates himself to us

☐

C. Once we become belivers then

1. We automatically grow in knowledge of God every year
2. We are able to begin to get to know God by using our spiritual abilities
3. There is nothing more to learn about God

☐

D. If God is our father and we are his children then

1. We can get anything we want from him
2. We ought to approach him with humility, fear and obedience
3. We need not bother any more how we live

☐

E. You can tell if people really know God by

1. The fact that they go to church regularly
2. The fact that they can preach
3. The attitudes of peace, courage and worship in their lives

☐

F. Knowing God personally will make me

1. Forget about other people and their needs
2. Very humble and thoughtful of the needs of others
3. Very pleased and proud of myself

☐

Now send your answers to: ....

They will be marked and returned to you in due course

THE DOCTRINE OF GOD

SUBJECT: THE LIVING GOD *Part 1*

COURSE 2
Lesson No. 3

SUBJECT: THE LIVING GOD – part 1

COURSE NO. 2
Lesson No. 3

IN LESSONS ONE AND TWO we saw:

evidence that God is and

how God may be known personally.

IN THIS LESSON we shall begin to answer the question:

what is this God like; what is his nature?

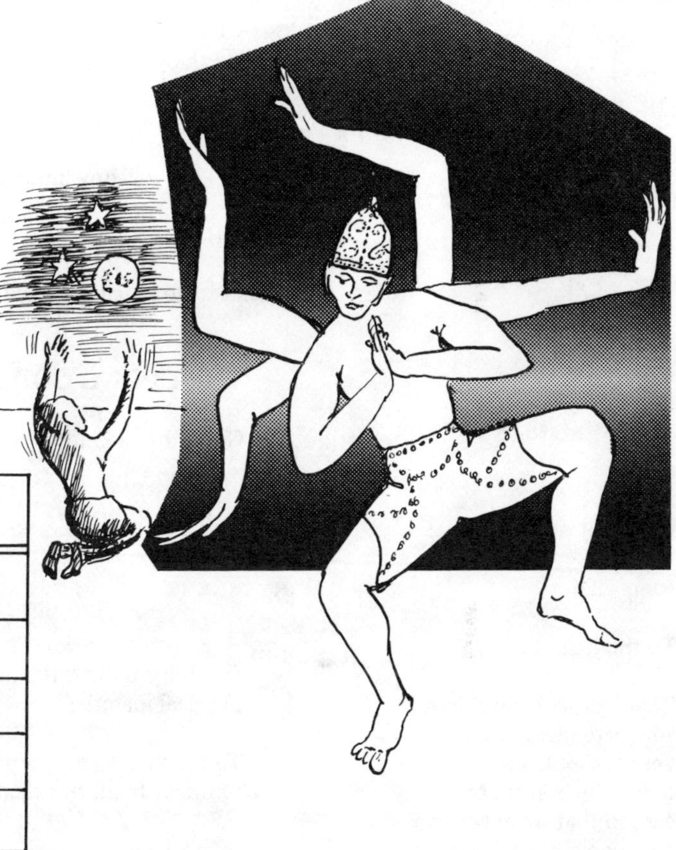

1. INTRODUCTION

Each of these verses includes a name of God. Write here the one name that is common to all the verses:

Deuteronomy 5:26 Joshua 3:10 I Samuel 17:26 Psalm 42:2

Daniel 6:26 Acts 14:15 II Corinthians 6:16 I Timothy 4:10

Eight people all describe God as "living God". Who are they?

1. Judges 8:19	5. II Chronicles 18:13
2. Ruth 3:13	6. Psalm 18:46
3. I Samuel 19:6	7. Jeremiah 4:2
4. I Kings 1:29	8. Jeremiah 38:16
"The living God"	

THE GOD OF THE BIBLE IS DIFFERENT FROM ALL FALSE GODS BECAUSE HE ONLY IS "THE LIVING GOD".

Check, then proceed:

The answers on page 1 should read like this:

The living God

Gideon	:	Micaiah
Naomi	:	Psalmist
Saul	:	Children of Israel
David	:	Zedekiah

All living things that we see on earth

(i) are made of physical material

(ii) occupy limited space and

(iii) become different as time passes

So what is God made of and how does he live?

The god of this world

2. THE LIVING GOD IS A SPIRIT BEING

God is not a kind of big man; he is not made of physical material.

Write out:

John 4:24

. . . .

. . . .

The Bible defines the nature of God as "spirit"; "spirit" must mean "not made of physical material".

To us, who do have a physical body, the idea of a Being who is simply spirit is difficult to understand. But there are certain things we must say . . .

To think about:

"Though we cannot have adequate ideas of God, yet we should endeavour to get the best that we can, so that we may serve and worship him, honour and glorify him, in the best manner . . ."
by Dr. John Gill (1697–1771) in his *Body of Divinity*.

God is Spirit. Therefore:

These three statements can be supported by the verses below:

1. God is invisible to us because we can only see physical material.
2. God does not have separate parts because he is one undivided Spirit.
3. God cannot be measured by time and space.

Look up these verses and put the correct number (from the statements above) in the boxes:

Deuteronomy 6:4		Exodus 33:20		Psalm 139:7–12	
John 10:30		I Timothy 1:17		Jeremiah 23:23, 24	

To think about:

"If God made man according to his image, we must raise our thoughts of God according to the noblest parts of man . . . We must conceive of him by the perfections of our souls . . . The Almighty Father of spirits is not inferior to his children".
Stephen Charnock, B.D. (1628–1680)
Discourses upon the Existence of God.

THERE ARE THREE IMPORTANT THINGS THAT WE MUST NOTE CAREFULLY NOW

A. Because God is so different from us, we cannot understand exactly how he does things. He therefore has to make his actions understandable to us by describing them *in our human terms.*
E.g. See I Peter 3:12 and Deuteronomy 8:3.

God knows what we say – therefore the Bible says *he has ears* that hear.

God knows what we do – therefore the Bible says *he has eyes* that see.

God can make us know – therefore the Bible says *he has a mouth* that speaks.
what he wants

THESE TERMS ARE THE WAY GOD DESCRIBES HIS CONTINUAL ACTIVITIES SO THAT WE CAN LEARN *WHAT* HE DOES. THEY DO NOT DESCRIBE *HOW* HE DOES THEM. GOD DOES NOT HAVE THESE PHYSICAL PARTS.

Check, then proceed: The answers on page 3 should be, from left to right: 2 : 1 : 3

Theophany
a manifestation of God to people by actual appearance granted to the Old Testament Patriarchs in temporary ways, later becoming permanently the shekinah glory in the Tabernacle and finally superseded by the incarnation of Jesus Christ.

B. Because God is so different from us, he could not be seen by us unless he appeared in some physical form. A spirit Being can appear in a physical form (THEOPHANY).

E.G.

1 Sometimes God appeared as an *angel*

2 Sometimes God appeared in a *fire*

3 Sometimes God appeared like a *majestic person* on a throne

4 Sometimes God appeared like a *dove*

Each of these verses refers to one of the examples above. Write a number in each square to say which example is meant by that verse:

	John 1:32
	Judges 13:21, 22
	Isaiah 6:1
	Exodus 3:2

GOD IS NOT REALLY LIKE THESE THINGS. NO MAN CAN SEE THE ACTUAL SUBSTANCE OF GOD, SO THESE FORMS WERE APPEARANCES MERELY TO ENABLE MEN TO LEARN THAT GOD *DOES* EXIST. THEY DO *NOT* DESCRIBE *HOW* HE EXISTS. GOD DOES NOT HAVE ANY PHYSICAL SHAPE.

Check, then proceed: The answers on page 4 should be, from top to bottom: 4 1 3 2

Read:

Deuteronomy 4:15–19

C. Because God is so different from us, it is not possible to make any image or picture of him. No physical object can represent him or help us worship him. We must only worship him "in spirit and truth" (John 4:19–24), i.e. not by physical activity alone.

Write out:

Deuteronomy 4:15, 16

. . . .

. . . .

. . . .

. . . .

. . . .

. . . .

. . . .

. . . .

. . . .

To think about:

"The imageless worship of Jehovah (see 8/3) announced not merely that he was greater than nature but that he was also unbound by it" . . .
H. L. Ellison, B.A.B.D.
Baker's Dictionary of Theology, 1960.

GOD, WHO IS SPIRIT, IS NOT TO BE KNOWN BY OUR LIMITED PHYSICAL SENSES BUT BY THE FACULTIES OF OUR SOULS MADE SPIRITUALLY ALIVE BY THE HOLY SPIRIT – i.e. by our awakened conscience, enlightened understanding and renewed will.

Write out:

I Corinthians 2:12

. . . .

. . . .

. . . .

. . . .

3. THE LIVING GOD IS A PERSON

Pantheism
the teaching that God is everything and everything is God; that God does not have a distinct existence.

God is not vague universal spirit; he is a distinct Person who thinks, feels, plans, carries out his purposes and can relate to others. Such activities are *only* true of a person; they cannot be said of a thing.

A. God feels.

Write the correct reference in each square:

Proverbs 6:16

Genesis 6:6

Revelation 3:19

I Kings 11:9

	GRIEF
ANGER	
	LOVE
HATRED	

To think about:

"The little word 'father' lisped in prayer by a child of God exceeds the eloquence of all the famed orators of the world".
Martin Luther
(1483–1546)

B. The relationships God makes show him to be a person.

E.g. Father with children –

Write out:

Galatians 3:26

. . . .

. . . .

(we shall study more of God's names in lesson no. 4)

C. The personal pronouns (he, him, his) are used of God throughout scripture.

THE LIVING GOD IS A SPIRIT BEING WHO IS ALSO A *PERSONAL* BEING. HE IS NOT AN UNFEELING FORCE.

Check, then proceed:

The correct answers on page 6 are:

Genesis 6:6 : GRIEF
ANGER : I Kings 11:9
Revelation 3:19 : LOVE
HATRED : Proverbs 6:16

Write out:

4. THE LIVING GOD IS A SELF-SUFFICIENT PERSON

John 5:26
(first half only)

. . . .

No-one created God. He did not have a beginning. He does not depend on anything outside himself for life. God existed when there was nothing else. That was possible because he is the source of himself. This self-sufficiency is not true of any other person or thing.

THREE THINGS FOLLOW FROM THIS:

Eternal means, in this study, having no beginning or end.

A. Because God has the source of his life within himself, he must be eternal.

Write out:

Psalm 90:2

. . . .

. . . .

. . . .

. . . .

. . . .

God will still be living when the world ends, as he was before the world began.

Write out:

Hebrews 1:12

. . . .

. . . .

. . . .

. . . .

B. Because God is eternal, he is not influenced by time. This means that his life does not have past or future. He sees both the past and the future as always present.

Write out:

II Peter 3:8

. . . .

. . . .

. . . .

Read:

Revelation 1:8

To the people in the car:
A is past, B is present, C is future.
BUT to the people in the aeroplane:
A, B and C are all seen at once.
Similarly God, unaffected by our time, can see all time as present.

Jehovah is a word made up from the four Hebrew consonants YHVH plus the vowels of the Hebrew word for "Lord". The Jews felt God was too holy for them to use his real name, so they made-up this substitute name.

In the Hebrew language, the consonants YHVH, used frequently of God, are probably derived from the verb 'to be'. This is certainly how God explained his name to Moses:

Write out:

Exodus 3:14
(first part only)

"I am" – 1st person of verb "to be".

. . . .

. . . .

Moses could be comforted by the fact that God is not merely One who was, nor merely One who will be; GOD IS ONE WHO *IS* WITH HIM *ALWAYS.*

The same truth can be a comfort to us also; every past experience we have of God teaches us what he will always be to us because his nature is unchanging.

Write out:

Deuteronomy 33:27
(first part only)

. . . .

. . . .

Immutable means his nature is always the same.

C. Because God has the source of his *life in himself* and since he is therefore *eternal,* it also follows that he is *immutable.* Because he is not dependent upon anyone for his life and since he is outside of time, there is nothing that can ever change him or cause him to grow old.

Write out:

Malachi 3:6 (first part only)

. . . .

Attribute means any quality which is essential to the nature of a person or thing. Wetness is an attribute of water. Heat is an attribute of fire. The ability to reason is an attribute of a human being.

God would cease to be God if he lost his truthfulness, his power, his love and his immutability. So these are some of his attributes.

GOD'S NATURE never changes Being holy he cannot improve Being perfect he cannot be incomplete	1	
GOD'S ATTRIBUTES never change His truthfulness, power and love never alter	2	
GOD'S PLANS never change His knowledge and power are perfect, so what he plans is always right and always possible	3	
GOD'S PROMISES never change because his plans never need changing	4	
GOD'S THREATENINGS never change His love of holiness and his hatred of sin never vary	5	

Write in the squares at the side, that reference from this list which applies to that square:

Jeremiah 31:3 Numbers 23:19 Matthew 25:41 James 1:17 Psalm 33:11

Check, then proceed:

The correct answers on page 9 are:

1 : James 1:17
2 : Jeremiah 31:3
3 : Psalm 33:11
4 : Numbers 23:19
5 : Matthew 25:41

N.B. God may sometimes change his *methods* without ever changing his *nature.*

Write out:

Jonah 3:10

. . . .

. . . .

. . . .

. . . .

. . . .

To think about:

"The divine immutability should not be understood as implying immobility, as if there were no movement in God . . . there is change round about him . . . in the relations of men to him but there is no change in his being, his attributes, his purpose, his motives . . . or his promises".
Prof. L. Berkhof (1873–1957)
Systematic Theology, p. 59.

GOD *ALWAYS* HATES SIN AND IS *ALWAYS* MERCIFUL TO THE PENITENT

So if the sinners whom God threatens repent of their sin, then God no longer threatens them but now graciously receives them. God has changed his *method* but not his *nature.* In reality, such a change is not in God but in the sinners and in God's relationship with them. If God destroyed a penitent people or saved unrepentant sinners, *that* would be a change in his nature.

GOD'S IMMUTABILITY MEANS THAT THE IDEA MUST BE WRONG THAT GOD WAITS TO SEE IF PEOPLE WILL ACCEPT HIM BEFORE HE DECIDES TO ELECT THEM AS HIS HOLY CHILDREN. HE CANNOT CHANGE HIS PURPOSES LIKE THAT. HE KNOWS WHOM HE HAS ELECTED FROM THE BEGINNING – see Ephesians 1:4, 5.

My name is .... My address is ....

QUESTIONS ABOUT LESSON 3

Only one answer is correct.
Put here the number of the correct answer.

A. The God of the Bible is not like false gods because	1. He is the God of the Jews only 2. He is the only living God 3. He does not require any offerings	☐
B. The fact that God is a spirit-being means that	1. We humans cannot know him at all 2. All our spirits are a part of him 3. He must reveal himself to us in special ways	☐
C. Since the living God is the only self-sufficient Being	1. The material of this world is not eternal 2. He cares for no-one but himself 3. We do not really exist at all	☐
D. Because God lives outside of time	1. He cannot give us the comfort we need 2. He sees our past, present and future all at once 3. He is not interested in us at all	☐
E. The unchanging nature of God means that he	1. Can never forgive our sins 2. Cannot keep up-to-date with our world 3. Always punishes sin and always forgives repentant sinners	☐
F. God decided to have me for his child only after waiting to see that I would repent and believe	1. This is true biblical teaching 2. This is a wrong idea; it is not what the Bible teaches	☐

Now send your answers to: ....

They will be marked and returned to you in due course

THE DOCTRINE OF GOD

SUBJECT: THE LIVING GOD *Part 2*

COURSE 2
Lesson No. 4

1. INTRODUCTION

IN OUR LESSONS SO FAR we have studied:

evidences that God exists

how to know God personally

what God is like

IN THIS LESSON we shall study the question:

where does God live?

Fill in the correct lesson number

We learned in lesson ☐ that God does not have physical parts; he is *spirit*.

A spirit Being will not be confined to any particular physical place. (Even we are free to "go" *in our thoughts* to many places).

It follows that God (who has no body) does not live in a particular physical place as we must do because we have physical bodies.

Write out:

Psalm 139:7, 8

. . . .

. . . .

. . . .

. . . .

. . . .

. . . .

. . . .

Check, then proceed: The correct lesson number on page 1, line 7, is: Lesson 3, page 2 section 2
Read it again!

Omniscience
knowledge of all things.
To be studied in lesson 7.

2. THE WHOLE OF GOD IS IN EVERY PLACE

This is clear from the following Bible statements:

A. God knows everything (OMNISCIENCE)

Write out:

Hebrews 4:13

. . . .

. . . .

. . . .

. . . .

B. God sustains everything

Write out:

Acts 17:28
(first part only)

. . . .

. . . .

Omnipotence
all powerful.
To be studied in lesson 9.

C. God controls everything (OMNIPOTENCE)

Write out:

Psalm 103:19

. . . .

. . . .

. . . .

Attributes
See – lesson 3
page 9

These three things are some of his attributes. Because he has them:

Omnipresence
See – page 4 of this lesson

D. The whole of God must be everywhere (OMNIPRESENCE)

Write out:

Jeremiah 23:24

. . . .

. . . .

. . . .

This means that he is not part here, and part there, but fully present everywhere.

3. THREE PROBLEMS

Look up:

Genesis 4:16
Numbers 14:43
Proverbs 15:29

A. Sometimes scriptures refer to people "going from the presence of God" or of God "not being with the wicked". How can these things be true if God is everywhere?

Answer: Because God does not have a physical body but is spirit, it is not possible to go a *physical* distance away from him. But it is possible for us to cease to have him in our thoughts. In that sense, people can go away from God.

B. If God is everywhere, how is there room for us?

Answer: Because God is a different kind of being from us, he can exist everywhere without our being physically conscious of him. (To try to illustrate this, the air in which we live is full of radio waves. We can only detect them with a radio. Otherwise we are not conscious of their existence because their nature is different from ours.)

C. If God is everywhere, he must be in places where wickedness and uncleanness exist; is he not thereby defiled?

Answer: God, who is spirit, cannot be defiled by physical pollution, as the rays of the sun are not dirtied by shining on mud. Because God is pure and holy, he cannot be defiled by moral pollution, as water and oil cannot mix.

Write out:

Isaiah 66:1

....

....

....

....

4. THREE FACTS ABOUT WHERE GOD IS

Omnipresent
present everywhere

A. The whole of God is in every place. This we have already proved (page 2). We can say that God is omnipresent.

Immensity
not limited by space

B. God is not confined within the space of our world. We can say that God has immensity.

Transcendent
unrealisable in natural experience

C. God may only be known if he wishes to be known. We can say that God is transcendent.

These three facts are taught in the Bible:

Write out:

Romans 11:33

. . . .

. . . .

. . . .

Which of the three facts above does this prove? Insert the correct letter:

☐

Write out:

Proverbs 15:3

. . . .

. . . .

. . . .

Which fact does this support? Write the correct letter:

☐

Write out:

Job 11:7 and 9

. . . .

. . . .

. . . .

. . . .

Which fact does this prove? Write the correct letter:

☐

Check, then proceed: The correct answers on page 4 are: Romans 11:33 [C] Proverbs 15:3 [A] Job 11:9 [B]

Pantheism
the doctrine that God is merely the sum total of all created things.
see – lesson 3
page 6

From what we have learned so far, we can see that Pantheism and Deism are wrong ideas. Pantheism denies *God's immensity and transcendence*

Deism
the doctrine that God does not enter into the affairs of men, but remains aloof.

Deism denies *God's omnipresence.*

5. **GOD REVEALS HIMSELF IN DIFFERENT WAYS** though he is everywhere present.

For example:

A. In heaven, God's glory is especially and visibly shown.

Write out:

Revelation 4:2

. . . .

. . . .

. . . .

Read:

Revelation 4:3–11

See also:

Acts 7:55, 56

Shekinah
a Hebrew word meaning "to dwell" or "presence".

B. In Old Testament days God was in the midst of his people and showed his presence by the shekinah glory in the tabernacle and temple.

Write out:

Exodus 40:34

. . . .

. . . .

. . . .

See also:

Isaiah 57:15

C. In these New Testament days God the Father and the Son make their home with believers by the Spirit.

Write out:

John 14:23

. . . .

. . . .

. . . .

D. In the new heavens and new earth God will dwell with all his people and his glory will be visible to them.

Write out:

Revelation 21:3

. . . .

. . . .

. . . .

. . . .

6. HOW GOD'S OMNIPRESENCE HELPS BELIEVERS

A. This truth is *a challenge* to believers

Write out:

Psalm 139:7–8

. . . .

. . . .

. . . .

So there is *nothing* hidden from God. We should understand that he sees every thought, word and act of ours, wherever we go and whenever we do them. This should make us careful in our behaviour.

See: Genesis 16:13
Jonah 1:4–17
II Samuel 12:9

HERE ARE THREE BIBLE PEOPLE WHO LEARNED THAT GOD KNEW EVERYTHING THEY DID. WHO ARE THEY?

ADDIV [ ] JOHAN [ ] GAHAR [ ]

Check, then proceed: The three names at the bottom of page 6 are: DAVID : HAGAR : JONAH

Read:

John 3:19, 20
II Kings 6:8–12

The Bible described ungodly people as living in darkness and as loving darkness because their deeds are evil; but God knows all that happens, even the secrets of the ungodly! If God sees the deeds of the ungodly in the dark, how much more will he see the deeds of believers!

Write out:

Psalm 139:2

. . . .

. . . .

This should make us careful in our behaviour.

B. The truth of God's omnipresence is *a comfort* to believers

Write out:

Psalm 23:4

. . . .

. . . .

. . . .

Wherever we go, we should understand that our God is there also. We are never alone. We can never move to where his presence is not. This should be a comfort to us.

See:

Genesis 5:22
Genesis 6:9

HERE ARE TWO BIBLE PEOPLE WHO CONTINUALLY WALKED WITH GOD EVERYWHERE THEY WENT. WHO ARE THEY?

HANO [ ]

CHENO [ ]

Read:

Psalm 46:1 and
Isaiah 43:1, 2

Check, then proceed: The two names at the bottom of page 7 are: NOAH ENOCH

God's presence everywhere means that he is in every event that happens and can work through every event for the spiritual good of his children.

Write out:

Romans 8:28

. . . .

. . . .

. . . .

. . . .

C. The knowledge of God's omnipresence *strengthens believers* in difficult situations.

Write out:

Matthew 28:20
(last part only)

. . . .

. . . .

Read:

II Timothy 4:16, 17
Exodus 33:14–16

The continual presence of Jesus Christ is a source of strength to believers as they seek to serve God everywhere by spreading the knowledge of the gospel. He of whom they speak is with them as they go!

DO YOU REALISE GOD IS WITH YOU AT THIS MOMENT ?

Then take time *now* to worship him and thank him in prayer.

My name is .... My address is ....

QUESTIONS ABOUT LESSON 4

Only one answer is correct. Put here the number of the correct answer.

A. We know that God *is* everywhere because

1. The Bible explains this truth to us
2. Christians have always said so
3. Scientists have detected his presence everywhere

☐

B. Since God is everywhere

1. Everyone can find him at any time
2. He can, if he wishes, show himself to anyone
3. There is no need to search for him at all

☐

C. People knew God was amongst them in Old Testament days because

1. Miracles kept happening for them
2. Nothing ever went wrong for them
3. God let them see some of the glory of his presence

☐

D. Christians know God is with them nowadays because

1. They have no troubles or illnesses
2. Because he says he is
3. They are victorious in all their troubles

☐

E. Because nothing is hidden from God's sight

1. We are encouraged to be careful in everything
2. We may as well not bother how we behave
3. He will know we are no worse than other people

☐

F. Since God is in control of everything

1. He can make everything bring blessing to us
2. We can blame him when things go wrong
3. We can expect to understand everything that happens to us

☐

Now send your answers to: ....

They will be marked and returned to you in due course.

THE DOCTRINE OF GOD

SUBJECT: THE LIVING GOD *Part 3*

COURSE 2
Lesson No. 5

SUBJECT: THE LIVING GOD – part 3

COURSE NO. 2
Lesson No. 5

1. INTRODUCTION

IN LESSONS 1–4 we have been learning about:

the existence and nature of God and that

true religion is a matter of being rightly related to this God.

IN THIS LESSON we are to learn what the Bible teaches about the way God and his people are related.

Write out:

Psalm 34:22

. . . .

. . . .

. . . .

A Christian is a person who has a relationship of trust in the living God.

Write out:

I Corinthians 6:19

. . . .

. . . .

. . . .

A Christian is a person who is the temple of the living God.

These two scripture verses teach that a true Christian has a very close relationship with the living God.
Let us examine this relationship more closely.

2. THE SIGNIFICANCE OF NAMES

A. In daily life the name of a thing or of a person often expresses the nature of that thing or person. (E.g. the name Chelmsford indicates that the town stands on the ford across the river Chelmer).

B. In the Bible a name is often used as a description of the person whose name it is.

PONTEFRACT

"broken bridge"

Write out:

Genesis 1:27

. . . .

. . . .

. . . .

This Hebrew word for "man" is first used in Genesis 1:27

In the Hebrew language one word for "man" (Genesis 1:27) is "adham". In Genesis 2:19, 20, 21 the man is called Adam which is the same word "adham" meaning "red". So the name Adam means "man" and "red coloured"; the name describes the person having it. "Adham" refers to man as a human person distinct from the animals.

Write out:

Genesis 2:23

. . . .

. . . .

. . . .

. . . .

BLACKWATER

This second Hebrew word for "man" is first used in Genesis 2:23

The Hebrew word here for "woman" is "ishshah"; the Hebrew word here for "man" is "ish". "Ish" refers to man as the male, distinct from the female. The word "ishshah" means "from ish", so "woman" describes the fact that she is "from man".

C. Scripture often gives the meaning of names and explains why those names were given:

Write in the meanings:

Genesis 3:20	EVE means
Genesis 5:29	NOAH
Exodus 2:10	MOSES
Matthew 1:21	JESUS
John 1:42	CEPHAS

Check, then proceed:

The correct answers at the end of page 2 are:

EVE	– (mother of all) LIVING
NOAH	– (This shall) COMFORT (us)
MOSES	– DRAWN OUT (of the water)
JESUS	– He shall SAVE (his people)
CEPHAS	– A STONE

---

3. THE SIGNIFICANCE OF THE NAMES OF GOD

A. God's names show us how he is related to his people. His names help them to understand what he does for them.

"YHWH" see – lesson 3 page 8

B. We shall concentrate on those names of God which are based on the Hebrew word "YHWH". (There are other names for God based on the Hebrew word "EL"). We keep to the group of names based on "YHWH" because they are the names especially used when talking of God's relationship to his people.

Names using the letters "YHWH" occur more than 6000 times in the Old Testament. Names linked with "EL" occur 2570 times. No other names for God are used so much as these two.

C. This name "YHWH" – often spoken as "Jehovah" – means "the one who always exists" or as in Exodus 3:14 "I AM THAT I AM".

The meaning is that GOD IS ALWAYS THERE, dependable, faithful, reliable. Because the Lord Jesus Christ is God, he also speaks of himself in this way. He says:

"I AM, I WAS, I WILL BE . . ."

Write out:

Revelation 1:8

. . . .

. . . .

. . . .

. . . .

"YHWH" is sometimes called God's "covenant" name because it is the name he uses when speaking of his relationship (covenant) with his people. Jehovah is always dependable and it is a precious thing when he makes covenants (agreements) with his people. His name means: "He always is what he promises to be!" That must be a joy to his people!

יְהוָֹה

YHWH

JEHOVAH

אֵל

EL

GOD

A - ΑΛΦΑ

ALPHA – BEGINNING OF GREEK ALPHABET

Ω - ΩΜΕΓΑ

OMEGA – END OF GREEK ALPHABET

4. SOME OF THE "JEHOVAH" NAMES OF GOD

A. *Jehovah-jireh, Genesis 22:14*

Read:

Genesis 22:1–14

The name means "The Lord who provides". This teaches us that God provides for the needs of his people. And this story of the ram caught in the bush illustrates the important truth that God provides the sacrifice necessary as a substitute for his people, as Abraham said . . .

Fill in the verse number where Abrahams says this:

GENESIS 22 verse ☐

This truth about God is a basic one. Once we know that God will provide, we can go on to build our lives on that good foundation.

B. *Jehovah-rophekah, Exodus 15:26*

Read:

Exodus 15:23–26

The name means "The Lord that heals". We learn here that God preserves his people. All health, spiritual and physical, comes from him either by his direct gift or by his working through other means.

C. *Jehovah-nissi, Exodus 17:15*

Read:

Exodus 17:8–16

This name means "The Lord my banner". Armies used to follow the flag into battle and gather around it as a place they knew was safe for them. So we learn that in the spiritual warfare of the Christian life believers can confidently "gather around" God.

Check, then proceed: The correct verse number is: Genesis 22 verse 8

D. *Jehovah-mekaddishkim, Exodus 31:13*

Read:

Exodus 31:12–17

This name means "The Lord that makes you holy". God is holy (we shall study this in lesson 6) and his people must be holy also. But God does not command us to be holy and then leave us to struggle by ourselves. He works with and in his people to make them holy.

Write out:

Philippians 2:13

. . . .

. . . .

. . . .

. . . .

E. *Jehovah-shalom, Judges 6:24*

Read:

Judges 6:11–24

This name means "The Lord who is peace". The story shows how God came to a frightened man and gave him courage and the promise of peace through victory.

F. *Jehovah-sabaoth, I Samuel 17:45*

Read:

I Samuel 17:42–51

The name Jehovah-sabaoth occurs 80 times in Jeremiah; 88 times in Haggai, Zechariah and Malachi.

The name David used here means "The Lord of hosts". David knew that his God was the God who had all power because he controlled all the angels, all human forces, all the powers of the universe and even the actions of all evil powers. This was a name of God much used when the Jews were being defeated and after their exile in Babylon. This name of their God gave courage to a small weak people.

G. *Jehovah-roih, Psalm 23:1*

Read:

Psalm 23

This name of God – "The Lord my shepherd" – teaches us that God personally guides, protects and cares for his people, just as a shepherd cares for his flock.

H. *Jehovah-zidkenu, Jeremiah 23:6*

Read:

Jeremiah 23:5–8

This name means "The Lord our righteousness". Jeremiah is prophesying of the Messiah who is to come to Israel – during Messiah's reign God's people will be saved and made righteous by him.

Write out:

I Corinthians 1:30

....

....

....

....

From this verse it is clear that Jesus Christ is the righteousness of all Christian believers. Jeremiah therefore was foretelling the coming of Christ in Jeremiah 23:6.

I. *Jehovah-shammah, Ezekiel 48:35*

Read:

Ezekiel 48:29–35

This name means "The Lord is there". The prophet is teaching that God is personally present with his people.

From these NINE ways in which the Old Testament describes Jehovah we learn the nature of God's relationship with his people; he provides for, heals, leads, sanctifies, gives peace to, powerfully supports, shepherds, gives righteousness to and dwells with all those to whom he is related. Do they include you?

5. FOUR MEN WHO ENJOYED A RELATIONSHIP WITH THIS LIVING GOD

Read:

Joshua 3:1–17

A. *Joshua* was able to assure the people that God could do wonders for them because the living God was related to them.

Write out:

Joshua 3:10
(first part only)

. . . .

. . . .

Read:

I Samuel 17

B. *David* was only a youth, yet because he knew the living God he had confidence to face the giant.

Write out:

I Samuel 17:26
(last part only)

. . . .

. . . .

Read:

II Kings 18:28–19:7

C. *Hezekiah* was besieged in the city and there seemed no hope of a victory against the Assyrians. But Hezekiah had a relationship with the living God and remarkable things happened.

Write out:

II Kings 19:4
(first part only)

. . . .

. . . .

. . . .

Read:

Daniel 6

D. *Daniel* was a prisoner in a foreign country. Yet his relationship with the living God was so strong that his witness brought blessing to the king and all the empire.

Write out:

Daniel 6:26

. . . .

. . . .

. . . .

. . . .

. . . .

6. THE SIN OF THINKING THAT GOD IS LIMITED LIKE A MAN

Write out:

Jeremiah 10:5

The NIV has an interesting translation of this verse.

. . . .

. . . .

. . . .

. . . .

. . . .

Living God
see – lesson 3
page 1

Jehovah is different from all man-made gods because he is THE LIVING GOD. Then let us not think of him as confined within limits as if he were a silent, powerless scarecrow in a melon patch!

Read:

I Kings 8:27

A. Do not think of God as limited to a building or to any special day. We may use a special building for worship on Sundays but we must also worship him in all places and on all days. Obey his word whenever you read it, not only on Sundays.

Read:

Hebrews 3:12

The early Jewish Christians were not to turn back because of thinking that God was only with the Judaism they had left.

B. Do not think of God as limited to your own church programme. Since God is the living God, his power can break out and do things in other places also. We cannot confine him to our work alone. We should be praying for the true work of God in every place. When we ask God to bless what we are doing, we should also ask him to show us what he is doing!

C. Do not think of God as limited to your own experience of him. Sometimes our own spiritual life is so low that we do not expect him to do for others anything more than he has done for us! Thinking like that is a sin – we should be hungry for him to do more with us – and with others.

Encouragement for God's People
to be derived from
His descriptive NAMES & TITLES
in the Old Testament.
יְהוָה: YAHWEH
(OR JEHOVAH)
GOD –
עֶלְיוֹן
Elyon
— MOST HIGH
צִדְקֵנוּ
Tsidkenu
— OUR RIGHTEOUSNESS
שָׁמָּה
Shammah
— IS THERE
שָׁלוֹם
Shalom
— OUR PEACE
צְבָאוֹת
Tsabaoth
— OF HOSTS
רֹעִי
Ro'oi
— MY SHEPHERD
יִרְאֶה
Jireh
— WILL PROVIDE
רֹפְאֶךָ
Ropheka
— YOUR HEALER
נִסִּי
Nissi
— OUR BANNER
מְקַדִּשְׁכֶם
Mekaddishkem
— YOUR SANCTIFIER
9/5

My name is .... My address is ....

QUESTIONS ABOUT LESSON 5

Only one answer is correct. Put here the number of the correct answer.

A. In the Bible the names of things	1. Have no real significance 2. Often tell us something about those things 3. May rarely mean something	☐
B. The name "YHWH" is the name of God	1. Most used in the Old Testament 2. Least understood by us 3. Used only in the New Testament	☐
C. The name Jehovah-jireh means	1. God is our healer 2. God will provide 3. God is our warrior	☐
D. The name Jehovah-sabaoth means	1. God is the Lord of hosts 2. God is the Lord of the Sabbath 3. God curses sinners	☐
E. God's covenant relationship with Hezekiah ensured the preservation of Jerusalem	1. Because God caused the giant to fall over 2. Because God caused the Assyrians to withdraw 3. Because God caused King Darius to repent	☐
F. Because God relates himself to believers	1. They can rejoice in God's character 2. God must be limited by their deficiencies 3. They need not pray any more	☐

Now send your answers to: ....

They will be marked and returned to you in due course

THE DOCTRINE OF GOD

SUBJECT: GOD IS HOLY

COURSE 2
Lesson No. 6

SUBJECT: GOD IS HOLY

COURSE NO. 2
Lesson No. 6

In the Old Testament, words for "holiness" occur over 800 times.

In the New Testament, words for "holiness" occur over 300 times.

One of the most common ideas found in the Bible is the idea of HOLINESS.

IN THIS LESSON we shall study what the Bible teaches about *the holiness of God.*

1. THE MEANINGS OF THE WORD "HOLINESS" IN THE OLD TESTAMENT

"... The usage of the Hebrew word clearly indicates as its central idea, that of separation..."
from a study by Prof. B. B. Warfield (1851–1921)

The Hebrew word meaning "holy" is the word "QADOSH". This word has come from another, older, word "QAD" which means "to cut" (and so, "to separate").

A. Originally, therefore, to say "God is holy" meant that God is absolutely distinct from all his creatures. He is separated from them, exalted above them, uniquely different from them.

Write out:

I Samuel 2:2

. . . .

. . . .

. . . .

God is different from all others because he is the only Being in existence who does not need any other being to support him. *Everything else depends on him for its existence* – God alone is truly self-contained and absolutely independent. This independence is what constitutes his God-ness; it is what gives him dignity and majesty above all others; it is what makes him alone the Holy One.

Write out:

Exodus 15:11

. . . .

. . . .

. . . .

"... the notion of a God cannot be entertained without separating from him whatever is impure ... to deny him purity is to make him a deformed, unlovely God ... he that saith, God is not holy, speaks much worse than he that saith, There is no God ..."
Stephen Charnock, B.D. (Puritan preacher, 1628–1680).

The meanings of the word "holiness" in the Old Testament (contd.)

B. The word "holiness" in the Old Testament also comes to include a further meaning. After the revelation of his law, in Exodus 20, it becomes clearer that God is not merely self-contained and so different from all creatures but he is also *separate from all sin and uncleanness.* Unlike everyone of us, God is always perfectly pure in his motives, acts, affections, thoughts and intentions. This infinite purity is the beauty of God; it is what gives him dignity and majesty above all others. Therefore this also is what makes him alone the holy one.

Write out:

I John 1:5 ....

....

....

C. The old Testament uses the word "holiness" of other things as well as of God. This happens when a thing is separated from other things, to be used only in God's service. Those things are *not holy in themselves.* They are holy only in the sense that *no-one but God is to have the use of them.* In this sense, God's people are "holy"; not because they are now sinless but because God has separated them for himself.

Write the correct verse in the space to which it refers:

holy ground	
holy nation	
holy day	
holy ointment	
holy gifts	
holy linen coat	

Exodus 3:5 19:6 28:38 30:25 35:2

Leviticus 16:4

Check, then proceed: The correct verses on page 2 are: holy ground, Exodus 3:5; holy day, Exodus 35:2; holy gifts, Exodus 28:38; holy nation, Exodus 19:6; holy ointment, Exodus 30:25; holy linen coat, Leviticus 16:4

---

2. THE HOLINESS OF GOD

"... God is oftener styled "holy" than "almighty" and is described by this part of his dignity more than by any other ..."
Stephen Charnock

A. We can now say that when the Bible speaks of God as holy, it means more than mere sinlessness. It means:

(i) He is distinct; set-apart; the only self-sufficient Being;
this is holiness *deriving from the uniqueness of God's nature.*

and (ii) He is entirely free from every moral and spiritual imperfection and is infinitely pure;
this is holiness *deriving from the perfection of God's behaviour.*

Read:

Isaiah 6:3 and
Revelation 4:8

B. Moreover, in the Bible "holy" is the word most used to describe God. The holiness of God is twice described in triple form as "Holy, holy, holy". No other adjective is used to describe God in this triple form. We must therefore say that holiness is the essence of God's beauty.

"... If the sun should lose its light, it would at the same time lose its heat and its life-giving virtue ... so, holiness is the splendour of every other attribute of God".
Stephen Charnock

Each of God's attributes is beautiful in its individual perfection, just as the individual parts of a flower are beautiful in themselves. Yet the parts of the flower have a special beauty when they are united together as a complete blossom. So the attributes of God have a special beauty that arises when we consider all his perfections united in the one divine nature. This *total beauty* constitutes God's unique holiness. We must say:

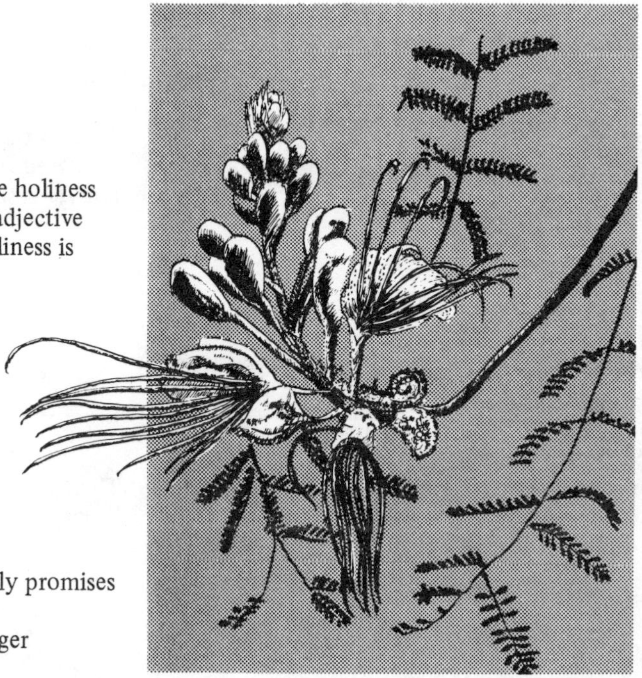

Attributes
see – lesson 3
page 9

God's justice is a holy justice

His wisdom is a holy wisdom

His power is a holy power

His promises are holy promises

His anger is holy anger

His name (i.e. his nature) is "Holy One".

Read:

Psalm 98:1 and
Psalm 105:42

Write out:

Isaiah 40:25

. . . .

. . . .

3. A HOLY GOD MUST HAVE A HOLY PEOPLE

God will not be related to a people who are unholy.

Write out:

I Peter 1:15, 16

. . . .

. . . .

. . . .

. . . .

As with God himself, so with his people, there are two senses in which we are to understand their holiness.

A. There is the primary sense; because God has chosen them to be his children God's people are thereby separated from other people. This is a *holiness of category.* They are regarded as perfectly holy though not yet actually so.

Write out:

I Corinthians 6:11
N.B. The verbs are all in the *past* tense; i.e. these things had already happened to them! *Sanctified* means made holy.

. . . .

. . . .

. . . .

. . . .

B. There is the secondary sense; the beauty of actual holiness. This can be seen in God's people as they become gradually holy by their striving with the Holy Spirit's power to live a life free from sin and obedient to God's commands. This is a *holiness of character.*

Write out:

Hebrews 12:14

. . . .

. . . .

NOTE THIS:

☞ IF THERE IS NO EVIDENCE OF ACTUAL HOLINESS IN PEOPLE'S LIVES (holiness in the *secondary* sense), THEN THERE IS NO PROOF THAT GOD HAS CHOSEN THEM (holiness in the *primary* sense).

4. HOW GOD SHOWS US THAT HE IS HOLY

As soon as God begins to relate himself to other creatures, the holiness which has always been his beauty now becomes evident in two ways:

A. Because he is God, he has the right to expect all others to obey him.
Because he is holy, his commandments are always right. God's commandments agree with his own holy nature. They show us what "rightness" is.

Write out

Psalm 145:17

. . . .

. . . .

Righteousness
the characteristic of God, expressing the rightness of all that he is and does.

The holiness of God shown in his commandments is called his *RIGHTEOUSNESS.*

B. Because God's commandments are right, it must be a sin to disobey them. Therefore, disobedience of God's commands rightly merits punishment. So God's punishments which indicate his hatred of sin are another expression of his essential holiness. Failure to obey God is an affront to the holiness of God and therefore must be wrong and deserves punishment. God's judgments show us how serious "wrongness" (sin) is.

Write out:

Deuteronomy 32:4

. . . .

. . . .

Justice
the characteristic of God, expressing his holiness by the righteous rewards and punishments which he attaches to his laws.

The holiness of God shown by his wrath is called his *JUSTICE.*

GOD'S LAWS --
EXODUS 20

NOTE THIS:

(i) We often demand that other people do things to please our personal wishes. God's righteous commands do not arise from any selfishness or pride in himself but from the fact that *his holiness always makes* him issue right commands.

(ii) We often judge other people and punish them out of passion or caprice. God's just punishments upon sinners do not arise from any passion or caprice in him but from the fact that *his holiness is right* when it is angry at sin.

Write out:

Isaiah 5:16

. . . .

. . . .

5. GOD'S HOLINESS SEEN IN THE GOSPEL MESSAGE

The fact that God's holiness is expressed by righteousness and justice makes the good news of the gospel so surprising. God can *save* sinners instead of punishing them *without being unjust!*

Write out:

Romans 3:26

. . . .

. . . .

. . . .

Because he is righteous, God can and does give men his laws to live by.
Because he is just, God must punish all who disobey these laws.
How then can God forgive sinners and still be righteous and just?

SURELY SINNERS CAN ONLY EXPECT PUNISHMENT FROM A JUST GOD?

Write out:

Romans 3:23

. . . .

. . . .

The sinner is without power to offer satisfaction for his sin himself. But Christ as God's appointed representative of sinners kept all God's laws on their behalf. Christ by his death also paid the price of the sins of all whom he represents. The gospel therefore is the surprising news that:

JESUS CHRIST HAS SATISFIED GOD'S RIGHTEOUSNESS AND JUSTICE *ON BEHALF OF ALL WHO BECOME BELIEVERS*

Write out:

Romans 3:24 and
I John 1:9

Confession of sin
to acknowledge to God that he has the right to make the laws we have broken, to punish us for the fact that we have broken them and to resolve that by his help we shall break them no more.

. . . .

. . . .

. . . .

. . . .

. . . .

Therefore God can still remain righteous and just and yet go on forgiving all who truly confess their sins to him.

6. THE HOLINESS OF GOD ILLUSTRATED

We will now study one passage in the Bible which contains essential teaching on the holiness of God, namely: Isaiah chapter 6 verses 1–8.

Write out:

Isaiah 6:1

. . . .

. . . .

. . . .

See II Chronicles 26.

King Uzziah died in a leper house. But during his reign the kingdom of Judah had risen to great prosperity and strength. By Uzziah's death as a leper, Isaiah is taught that earthly glory does not last. In contrast, God is seen as a holy king whose throne is everlasting.

Write out:

Isaiah 6:2–3

. . . .

. . . .

. . . .

. . . .

. . . .

. . . .

Seraphim
the word means "burning ones". They are personal, spirit beings.

". . . Much of modern preaching is anaemic . . . the life-blood of God's nature is absent from it . . . many evangelists centre their message on man . . . but the gospel of Christ is very different. It begins with God and his glory . . ."
W. J. Chantry, *Today's Gospel* (1970)

Notice the effect of the beauty of God's holiness *on the seraphim.*

Awe.	God's purity is so glorious that even sinless beings cannot look directly at it.
Humility.	They cover the lower part of their bodies as a mark of respect.
Obedience.	They are ready to fly at once on any errand for God.
Worship.	They continually speak of the distinguishing beauty of God's holiness.

NOTE THIS:

☞ Since these sinless creatures were so profoundly respectful to God, surely we who are sinners should be even more so? We should not come "TO CONSIDER" GOD'S WORD as though it was one among many others. We should not come glibly "TO WORSHIP" THIS GOD as though we do him a favour.

Write out:

Isaiah 6:5

. . . .

. . . .

. . . .

. . . .

". . . Today we are told that witnessing is to begin with 'God loves you' . . . The truth is that God is holy . . ."
W. J. Chantry, *Today's Gospel*

Notice the effect of the beauty of God's holiness on the prophet.

He was immediately conscious of his sinnership. He felt a sudden sense of the calamity he was in – he *ought* to be praising God like the sinless seraphs but as a sinner how could he? His situation left to himself was *hopeless*. "Woe is me!"

He knew he could not satisfy such a God unless he could somehow be cleansed and forgiven from his sin. "Undone" (AV) or "ruined" (NIV) mean "cut off". The prophet was *helpless* to change his situation.

Write out:

Isaiah 6:6

. . . .

. . . .

. . . .

Notice that cleansing and forgiveness came from the altar. The altar was the place where sacrifices were offered as substitutionary payment for sins of the worshipper. Here is a symbolic act which is prophetic of the salvation purchased by Christ by his death for those for whom he was the substitute.

Write out:

Isaiah 6:8

. . . .

. . . .

. . . .

". . . Preaching several easy steps to heaven is not evangelism . . . Paul preached a thorough-going theology, not a denuded four steps to eternal life . . ."
W. J. Chantry

The prophet is now able to respond and ready to serve this holy God. Since his ministry was to leave men worse than he found them (see verses 9, 10), the prophet would need this vision of God to keep him faithful in the hard task. *God's holy* glory is the source of his servant's strength!

THE UPWARD VISION (VERSE ONE) PLUS THE INWARD VISION (VERSE FIVE) COME BEFORE AN OUTWARD VISION (VERSE EIGHT) AND GIVE US AN ENDURING VISION (VERSE ELEVEN)

My name is .... My address is ....

QUESTIONS ABOUT LESSON 6

Only one answer is correct.
Put here the number of the correct answer

A. God's holiness arises from the fact that	1. He is not a man 2. He is unique among all creatures 3. He lives in heaven	☐
B. God's holiness is best thought of as	1. One of his many characteristics 2. The expression of his love 3. The total beauty of all his attributes	☐
C. God's laws are righteous because	1. They express his holy nature 2. They are for our good 3. They can be proved to be wise	☐
D. For God to punish those who disobey his laws is just because	1. God can punish anyone without reason 2. God's laws are right; to disobey them must therefore be wrong, justly punishable 3. Justice means punishment	☐
E. Because God is holy, those who are his people	1. Can leave him to make them holy somehow or other 2. Will spend much time talking about holiness 3. Will struggle to become holy too	☐
F. God's holiness is one of the things that	1. Makes him different from all man-made gods 2. Makes him like all other gods 3. Makes him lovable to us	☐

Now send your answers to: ....

They will be marked and returned to you in due course

THE DOCTRINE OF GOD

SUBJECT: GOD HAS A PLAN *Part 1*

COURSE 2
Lesson No. 7

1. INTRODUCTION

To think about:

"... Woe be to the people where the pulpit gives no utterance to the deep things of God; they will grow lean from want of nourishment and sad from lack of comfort."
C. H. Spurgeon (1834–1892), from his introduction to the textbook *'God's Sovereignty'* used in his Pastors' College

WE HAVE ALREADY LEARNED that God is:

a living Spirit-Person
eternal and everywhere present
powerful to control all things and
unique and holy.

Such facts lead us to expect that this God *will have a Plan for all things.*

NOW WE SHALL STUDY:

what the Bible teaches about God's Plan.

(N.B. This lesson may cause some questions to arise in your mind. The *next* lesson will study some of these questions.)

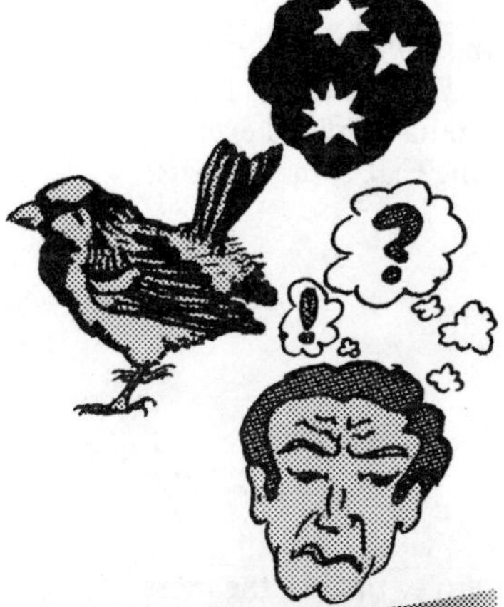

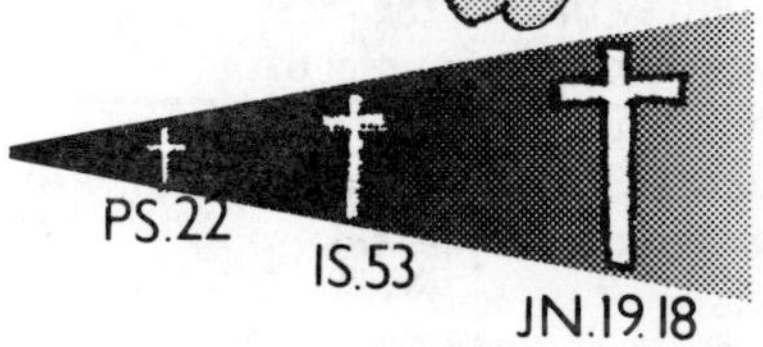

PS.22
IS.53
JN.19.18
.... INCLUDES EVERYTHING....

2. GOD'S KNOWLEDGE

Write out:

Job 37:16 ....
....

God's knowledge is perfect; i.e. it includes everything. For example:

Look up:

Look up		FILL IN THE MISSING WORDS	
Psalm 147:4	________	God knows every	
Matthew 10:29	________	God knows every	
Psalm 139:2	________	God understands our	
Isaiah 46:10	________	God declares things that are	
Psalm 81:13–14	________	God knows what things	might have happened

SINCE GOD ALWAYS KNOWS THE FUTURE SO FULLY, SURELY HE MUST HAVE PLANNED IT?

Check, then proceed:	The correct answers are:	God knows every	star
		God knows every	sparrow
		God understands our	thoughts
		God declares things that are	not yet done

3. NAMES GIVEN TO GOD'S PLAN

Predestination
the Bible teaching that God has planned everything that comes to pass.

In the Old Testament God's Plan is called:

His purpose	Isaiah 46:11
His pleasure (will)	Isaiah 53:10
His decree	Psalm 2:7

In the New Testament God's Plan is called:

His counsel (purpose)	Acts 2:23
His will	Ephesians 1:11
His eternal purpose	Ephesians 3:11

"... God, from all eternity did, by the most wise and holy counsel of his own will, freely and unchangeably ordain whatsoever comes to pass ..."
(from the Westminster Confession of Faith, 1647)

The Plan of God has been described as follows:

> "God has decreed in himself before the world began, by his most holy, wise and sovereign will, all things whatsoever that come to pass".
> (From the Strict Baptist "Affirmation of Faith", 1966)

NOTE THIS:

 Suppose it was NOT true that God has a Plan: to deny his Plan is to open wide the door to blind fate and mere chance! What peace, what refuge, could we then ever have in trials?
HOW THANKFUL WE SHOULD BE FOR THE REVELATION IN THE BIBLE THAT THERE IS BEHIND ALL THINGS A PLAN DEVISED BY A WISE AND HOLY GOD!

4. WHAT GOD'S PLAN IS LIKE

To think about:

"... God could not foreknow that things would be, unless he had decreed they should be."
Jonathan Edwards (1703–1758), a Puritan preacher.

There are five things we can say about God's Plan:

it is free
it is wise
it includes all things
it is eternal
it is gracious

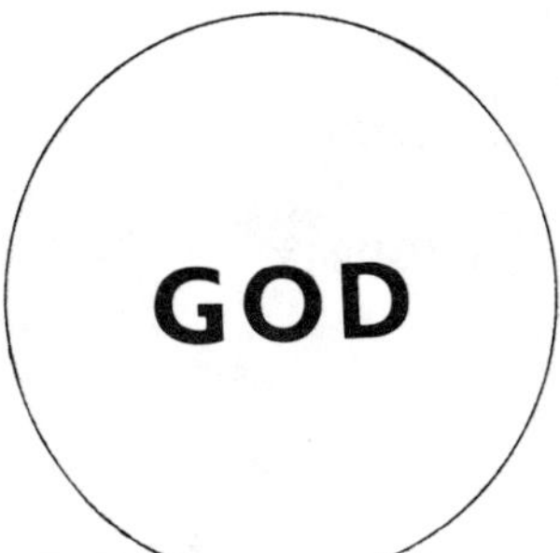

A. *God's Plan is free*

Independent
see – lesson 6 page 1

Holiness
see – lesson 6 page 3

Because God is not *dependent* on any other person for his life or welfare, there is no other who can ever influence or control him. He is free, unhampered by anyone or anything outside himself. Therefore no-one compelled him to make any Plan.

Because God is *free from any imperfection,* he is never forced to do anything because of a lack in himself or to supply a need for himself. He already IS all he needs to be. So God is:

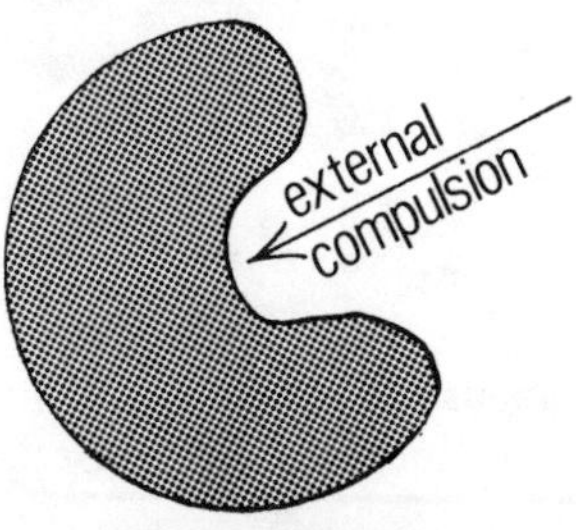

free from any external compulsion and
free from any internal constraint

Free
not in the power of any other

His Plan is the *free expression of his own will and pleasure.*

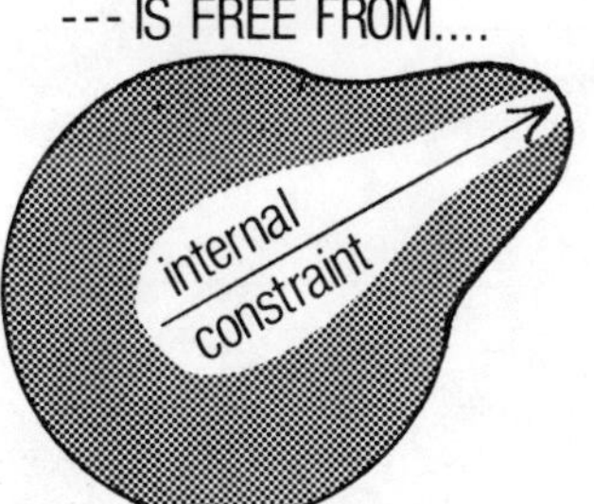

Write out:

Ephesians 1:11

. . . .

. . . .

. . . .

. . . .

. . . .

B. *God's Plan is wise*

Wisdom
the right use of knowledge.

God has perfect knowledge. But more importantly he also has "manifold wisdom" (Ephesians 3:10). The Greek word for "manifold" means literally "multi-coloured" or "full of many splendours".

Write out:

Psalm 104:24

. . . .

. . . .

. . . .

Because God has all knowledge PLUS having a wisdom which is full of capability to meet all situations must mean that his Plan is superbly right. There can be nothing unthinking or careless in it. IT IS VERY IMPORTANT TO KNOW THIS.

There will be much of God's Plan we will not understand. We must judge it all by the little we know. What we know is that the Plan must be right even when we do not understand it because God is so wise.

Write out:

Romans 11:33

. . . .

. . . .

. . . .

. . . .

C. *God's Plan includes all things that happen*

This must be so because each thing that happens is connected with other things that happen. If God's Plan does not include all things, he cannot have any plan! You cannot make a thing unless you have *everything* needed to make it.

God's Plan includes all things that happen (contd.)

For example, from the Bible we can see that God's Plan includes:

Write the correct Bible reference against each of the statements

	Statement	Reference		Bible references
1	The good works of men			Acts 18:9–11
2	The wicked deeds of men			Ephesians 1:4
3	Events in the history of the Jews			Acts 17:26
4	The progress of gospel preaching			Genesis 50:20
5	How long a man lives			Ephesians 2:10
6	The areas where nations live			Acts 2:23
7	Who will be a Christian believer			Job 14:5

D. *God's Plan is eternal*

Write out:

Acts 15:18

. . . .

. . . .

ALL THINGS

Since God's knowledge and wisdom are perfect, his Plan cannot have mistakes in it and therefore it never needs alteration or addition.

Eternal
see – lesson 3 page 7

Since God is eternal, he has always known what his Plan would be even before the world began. What happens now, God has always intended.

It follows that God's Plan is certain; no unexpected circumstance can ever arise to disturb it.

Write out:

Isaiah 46:10
(last part only)

. . . .

. . . .

Check, then proceed: The correct answers on page 5 are:

1. Ephesians 2:10
2. Acts 2:23
3. Genesis 50:20
4. Acts 18:9–11
5. Job 14:5
6. Acts 17:26
7. Ephesians 1:4

E. *God's Plan is gracious*

Read: Genesis 8:21

The fact that God should bother to design a Plan at all is gracious. God did not need to create a world. But he has created it although he knew we would disobey him. Surely we must admit that God is *surprisingly gracious*!

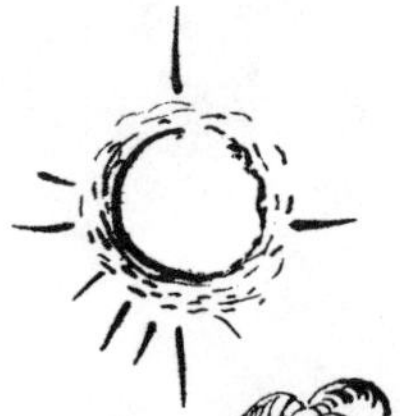

Write out: Genesis 8:22

Saint a born-again believer

. . . .

. . . .

. . . .

Even more surprising is the fact that God's Plan includes the special purpose of making sinners into saints and so creating the Christian church. To make rebellious people into his own children must be the *most gracious of all God's acts*!

Write out: Ephesians 1:11

. . . .

. . . .

. . . .

From this scripture verse it is clear that God himself chooses those who are to have the inheritance of being sons of God.

To think about:

"... The benevolent purpose that we should be holy, sons of God, destined to glorify him, is fixed, being part of a larger Plan embracing the universe ... hence nothing can upset the elect's future glory ..."

Dr. W. Hendriksen
Commentary on Ephesians 1:4–12 (1967)

GENESIS 8:22

5. ELECTION

From beginning to end the scriptures show us that the living God makes choices among men in carrying out his purposes. Abel, not Cain; Noah and family, and no-one else; Abram and family, not other citizens of Ur; Jacob, not Esau; Israel, not any other nation; the twelve disciples of Jesus; Saul not any other Pharisee, to be the apostle to the Gentiles, etc.

Read:

Matthew 11:25
John 17:2
Romans 9:14–18
I Corinthians 1:27–28
Ephesians 1:4–12
II Thessalonians 2:13

It is not strange therefore that when it comes to the creation of the Christian church (which is the supreme purpose of the Plan) God is clearly shown to choose who shall be his children and how they shall become his children in every detail.

Write out:

I Thessalonians 1:4

. . . .

. . . .

Peter encourages believers to be sure about their election by God:

Write out:

II Peter 1:10

. . . .

. . . .

. . . .

..God makes choices...

God's choice of his children:

Write the correct Bible reference against each of the statements

1	Is his own free choice		Romans 8:29–30
2	Once made is never altered		Ephesians 1:4
3	Makes their salvation certain		I Peter 1:2
4	Is not because of their faith		Romans 9:18
5	Is that they might be holy		Acts 13:48
6	Is that they might be obedient to Jesus		Romans 11:29

Check, then proceed: The correct answers on page 7 are:

1. Romans 9:18
2. Romans 11:29
3. Romans 8:29–30
4. Acts 13:48
5. Ephesians 1:4
6. I Peter 1:2

Election (contd.)

It is clear from the scriptures that God does not choose everybody to be members of his church. When he chose his people, he left others unchosen with their sins unforgiven. The Bible does not tell us why God chose some and left others unchosen but it does teach the fact.

Write out:

I Peter 2:8

. . . .

. . . .

. . . .

. . . .

God does not leave people unchosen merely because they are sinners for we *all* are such. Since God's Plan is based on his knowledge and his wisdom (see page 4), whatever he has done must be right even though we do not understand. We can say that:

those who are not chosen may nevertheless enjoy all the good things of this life.

their sinfulness is their own choice. They are not compelled to sin by God. Their condemnation is due to their own sinfulness.

many of them do hear the gospel and yet deliberately reject it.

if God in his mercy has chosen us to be his children, it is clearly not because of any reason in us. We are not better than those not chosen; indeed, we may have been worse sinners! We can only worship this God in humble astonishment, gratitude and devotion.

Write out:

Romans 11:36

. . . .

. . . .

My name is .... My address is ....

QUESTIONS ABOUT LESSON 7

Only one answer is correct. Put here the number of the correct answer.

A. Because God's knowledge is perfect	1. He knows only what has happened in the past 2. He always knows everything that happens 3. He knows certain things very accurately	☐
B. We say God's Plan is free. This means	1. We do not have to pay money for it 2. It only applies to free people 3. He is not compelled to make a Plan	☐
C. We say God's Plan is wise. This means	1. Only the wise people can understand it 2. It is too difficult for anyone to understand it 3. His Plan is perfectly just and right	☐
D. The Bible teaching about God's Plan must mean that	1. It includes everything that happens everywhere 2. It includes only religious things 3. It includes only large events of history	☐
E. We say God's Plan is gracious. This is because	1. He saves us although we are sinners deserving wrath 2. He is very gentle in his ways 3. His Plan is for gracious people	☐
F. God chooses certain people to be his children	1. Because of their faith 2. Because of their good deeds 3. Because he wishes to do so	☐

Now send your answers to: ....

They will be marked and returned to you in due course

THE DOCTRINE OF GOD

SUBJECT: GOD HAS A PLAN *Part 2*

COURSE 2
Lesson No. 8

SUBJECT: GOD HAS A PLAN – part 2

COURSE NO. 2
Lesson No. 8

IN LESSON SEVEN we learned:

> that God's Plan has always included everything that actually happens in the world and
>
> that God's Plan is wise, sovereign and gracious and certain to be fulfilled because he is a wise, gracious God.

Some people have serious questions in their minds when they try to understand this Bible teaching that God has a plan. This lesson will try to answer five of these questions.

QUESTION 1

Is not this teaching that everything happens according to God's previously fixed plan the same as the heathen idea of fatalism?

We answer: GOD'S PLAN IS VERY DIFFERENT FROM FATALISM

Fatalism says that:

> the world is a kind of machine which has somehow started to function by using only the various physical forces contained in it;
>
> there is no other reason behind events that happen;
>
> there is no good design being worked-out through events that happen;
>
> everything that happens is merely the relentless result of the inter-working of impersonal powers; and
>
> we are helpless to change the way this cosmic machine works.

THE BIBLE TEACHING ABOUT GOD'S PLAN IS VERY DIFFERENT

To think about:

"... A common charge against Calvin was that he introduced to Christianity the teaching of fatalism. Calvin repudiated this, pointing out that the doctrine (of God's Plan) rested on the will of a personal God who was perfect in wisdom, goodness, holiness, justice, and love ..."
from *The Teaching of Calvin* by A. M. Hunter, M.D., D. Litt. (1950)

To think about:

"... This is indeed graphic literature. It shows us man richly endowed, living in the midst of marvellous things – yet finding nothing in them. He is starved, homeless, despairing – because he forgets God..."
from *Commentary on the Bible book Ecclesiastes*, by G. Campbell Morgan, D.D. (1863–1945)

One of these verses will apply to one of the four Bible statements. Put the correct reference in each square.

There are four reasons why God's Plan is *not* the same as *Fatalism.*

FATALISM – says:	GOD'S PLAN – the Bible says:
Everything that happens is the effect of unintelligent natural forces.	God has wisely and lovingly planned everything that happens.
There is no special final event to which all things are moving.	God has planned everything to result in his glory.
Our human choices and actions cannot alter events.	God's Plan actually makes use of human actions for the good of his people.
We cannot be held responsible for what we do and can only despair for our future.	We are responsible for what we do, even though what we do is in God's Plan.

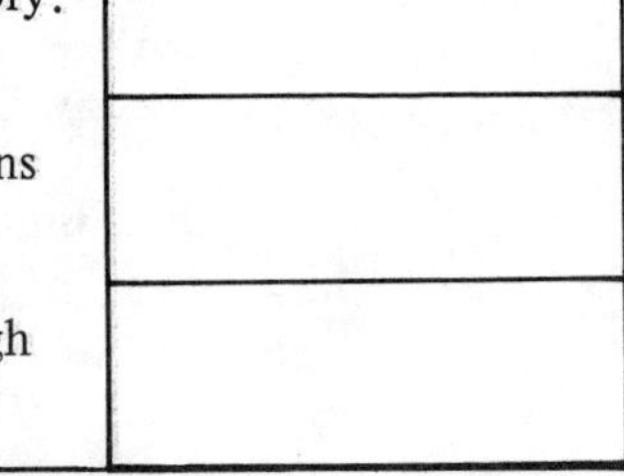

FATALISM FORGETS GOD!

Revelation 4:11 Ezekiel 18:20

Genesis 50:20 Acts 17:24–26

Check, the proceed: The correct answers on page 2 are: 1. Acts 17:24–26 2. Revelation 4:11 3. Genesis 50:20 4. Ezekiel 18:20

QUESTION 2

Free-will
The idea that a person can choose freely to do spiritual good. This is not the teaching of the Bible.

If everything that happens is already in God's Plan and therefore is certain to happen, then people are not free to decide how to act; so how can they be held responsible for their actions? Does not this teaching make people into puppets?

We answer: PEOPLE ARE RESPONSIBLE FOR WHAT THEY DO

There are two important points to be understood as we answer this question.

A. "Free-will" can only mean freedom to act *according to one's own nature.* No-one is absolutely free.

Write out:

John 8:34

. . . .

. . . .

. . . .

Here Jesus makes it clear that people are slaves to their own sinful natures. So as long as they act according to their natures, they feel they are acting freely. They are not in fact completely free. But they are not aware of any force compelling them to act because they can behave as they want to. A more accurate term to describe people's real state would be "self-will" rather than "free-will".

PEOPLE ARE ALWAYS UNDER THE CONTROL OF THEIR OWN CHARACTERS. THEY ARE PUPPETS OF THEIR OWN NATURES! THEREFORE PEOPLE CAN BE HELD RESPONSIBLE FOR WHAT THEY DO.

Question 2 (contd.)

B. The Bible teaches both (a) God's Plan includes all things and
(b) People are responsible for what they do.

Write out:

Jeremiah 25:11

(a) ....

....

Jeremiah knew the coming captivity was certain. Yet the Chaldeans were doing what they wanted to do when they captured Israel. They acted quite "freely".

Read:

John 19:23–37

In John 19 there are 4 verses which indicate that God's previously fixed Plan included actions that people "freely" carried out.

Write in the verse numbers which show God's Plan included people's "free" actions:

☐ ☐ ☐ ☐

Write out:

Acts 2:23

(b) ....

....

....

The crucifixion was certainly in God's Plan. Yet the Jews are called "wicked" because what they did was an evil thing. They *were* responsible.

See:

Matthew 26:75
Matthew 27:4

Peter wept for his sin of denying Jesus. Judas said: "I have sinned". Both men knew they were responsible for what they did, yet their deeds were all in God's Plan.

NOTE THIS:

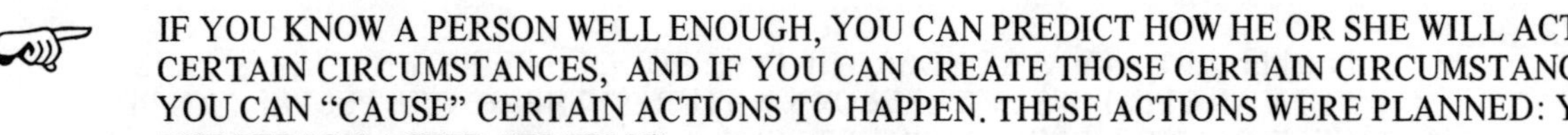

IF YOU KNOW A PERSON WELL ENOUGH, YOU CAN PREDICT HOW HE OR SHE WILL ACT IN CERTAIN CIRCUMSTANCES, AND IF YOU CAN CREATE THOSE CERTAIN CIRCUMSTANCES, YOU CAN "CAUSE" CERTAIN ACTIONS TO HAPPEN. THESE ACTIONS WERE PLANNED: YET THE PERSON ACTED "FREELY".

God knows us perfectly. God governs all circumstances. His plan therefore can include all our "free" actions. Yet we *still* are responsible because our actions arise "freely" from our own nature.

Check, then proceed: The correct verses on page 4 are: verse 24 : verse 28 : verse 36 : verse 37

QUESTION 3

To say that the evil things that happen are in God's Plan makes him the author of sin, does it not?

We answer: GOD IS NOT THE AUTHOR OF SIN

Holiness of God
see – lesson 6

The Bible teaches that God is perfectly holy; it cannot be possible for him to sin.

Write out:

Psalm 92:15

. . . .

. . . .

Nevertheless, sin and evil are in this world which is governed by God's Plan. God obviously allows people to behave in sinful ways. Since he is holy and good, he must have holy and good reasons for what he permits. This does not make him the author of these sins. People sin because their evil natures cause them to sin; God permits those sins only because his goodness and power can use them for good. He will not permit what he cannot use.

Write out:

Psalm 76:10

. . . .

. . . .

To think about:

"... God wills that men should do what they will, even if it is not what he would wish."
from *Difficulties in Christian Belief*, by A. C. MacIntyre, Ph.D. (1959)

Bible examples of God using evil for his good purposes

Write the correct verse against each of these four statements:

1.	Pharaoh was permitted to defy God in order that God's glory should be known more widely.	
2.	Saul sinned by committing suicide but that death was a just punishment by God.	
3.	God used Assyria to punish hypocritical Israel; yet Assyria acted "freely", delighting in war.	
4.	The crucifixion of Christ was a wicked act but was also the Father's will for his Son.	

Exodus 9:16 Isaiah 10:5, 7 Matthew 26:39 I Chronicles 10:13–14

Check, then proceed: The correct answers on page 5 are:

1. Exodus 9:16
2. I Chronicles 10:13–14
3. Isaiah 10:5, 7
4. Matthew 26:39

QUESTION 4

If God's plan includes everything and makes everything certain to happen, why need we bother to do anything ourselves?

We answer: WE MUST ALWAYS DO WHAT WE OUGHT

God's plan includes all things.
see – lesson 7
page 4

This question shows a failure to understand what God's plan is like. God's plan does not merely include the end-results of things; it includes all the causes of things, too. If the causes were not present, the end-results would not be achieved.

Write out:

Acts 18:10, 11

. . . .

. . . .

. . . .

. . . .

. . . .

God determined to save many people in Corinth; but he also determined that he would do so by using Paul's preaching.

Write out:

Daniel 9:2, 3

. . . .

. . . .

. . . .

. . . .

. . . .

. . . .

Daniel knew the end of the captivity was near. So he sets himself to pray for it. GOD WORKS HIS ENDS BY MEANS OF HIS PEOPLES' PREACHING AND PRAYING.

QUESTION 5

Election
see – lesson 7
page 7

Is not God unjust if his plan only makes certain the salvation of some people and leaves others in their sin?

We answer: GOD IS NOT UNJUST

Injustice means "to deny to anyone what they really deserve".

Write out:

Romans 3:23

. . . .

. . . .

To think about:

" . . . Does God hinder men from wanting to come to Christ? God forbid! . . . The devil hinders them: (II. Cor. 4:4); their own fallen nature hinders them: (I Cor. 2:14) . . .
from *Moral Difficulties of the Bible* (1941) by H. E. Guillebaud, M.A.

God is dealing with a sinful human race, every member of which deserves his wrath *because of their sin.* So by leaving them in their sin God is not unjust! He is *justly* leaving them to what they deserve!

If *one* child is chosen from an orphanage and adopted as a son in another family, is that family unjust because they do not adopt all the children from the orphanage?

Write out:

Romans 1:19, 20

. . . .

. . . .

. . . .

. . . .

. . . .

. . . .

GOD IS ABSOLUTELY FAIR – we can all see the evidence that God exists by the world in which we live.

Write out:

Romans 2:15

. . . .

. . . .

. . . .

GOD IS ABSOLUTELY FAIR – even Gentiles who do not have the law of Moses have a God-given conscience *within them* to guide them.

Write out:

Romans 10:8

. . . .

. . . .

. . . .

GOD IS ABSOLUTELY FAIR – the gospel message is preached widely throughout the whole world. No-one compels sinners to reject it. So if people do not believe the gospel, it is because they do not want to believe it.

To think about:

1. "Conversion and salvation must, in the very nature of the case, be wrought . . . either by ourselves alone; or by ourselves and God together; or solely by God himself. Pelagians believe the first; Arminians the second; true believers are for the last, because that is built on the strongest evidence of scripture, reason and experience".
   from "The Doctrine of Absolute Predestination"
   by Professor J. Zanchius (1516–1590)

A quote from a sermon by
Charles Haddon Spurgeon (1834–1892)

2. One day I said to myself: "I have believed in Jesus Christ and have passed from death unto life. To God be praise!" Then: "How have I come to be in this condition? Did I make this change in myself? No. Must I praise my own free will? No. Was there originally in me some betterness which led me to Christ while my companions have not come?"
   I dared not say so. I perceived that the difference was made by the sovereign grace of God. If the Lord saved me, then He intended to save: He did not do so by accident or inadvertence. There could be no reason why that intention should begin at any one moment; He must have purposed to save me from all eternity.

Notes:

1. Pelagius a British monk (about 400 AD) taught that people were able of themselves to keep God's commands and that God's grace was not really necessary.
2. Jacob Arminius (1560–1609) a Dutch theologian taught that people can use or refuse as *they* wish the grace God offers everyone.

FINAL COMMENTS

A. There is much about the Plan of God that we cannot expect to understand. The nature of God is so far above our human understanding that we shall always find sacred mysteries in our study of him. "There is no searching of his understanding" (Isaiah 40:28). He would not be God if mere humans could understand him!

Write out:

Deuteronomy 29:29

B. ....

....

....

....

We must always understand that the will of God must be thought of in two ways:

– his secret will, which is his total Plan known only to himself
– his revealed will, which is that part of his Plan that he has made known to us in the scripture.

Our duty is to obey the scripture and accept whatever that teaches about God.

Write out the last sentence of Genesis 18:25

C. ....

It is unthinkable that the God of the scriptures who gave his only Son to die for sinners could ever be unjust, unloving, unwise or unrighteous. Therefore where we cannot understand we worship in faith and humility.

My name is .... My address is ....

QUESTIONS ABOUT LESSON 8

Only one answer is correct.
Put here the number of the correct answer.

A. Fatalism is a wrong idea because	1. People themselves cause things to happen 2. It ignores the fact of God's rule over all things 3. Not many people believe it	☐
B. Free-will is a wrong idea because	1. We can only act according to what our nature is 2. Many people live under oppressive governments 3. We often do not know what to do	☐
C. When people sin it is because	1. God makes them 2. They obey their sinful natures 3. God cannot prevent them	☐
D. God's plan for the world includes	1. Everything that happens from beginning to end 2. Only the last things that are to happen 3. Only those things that are religious	☐
E. God is not unjust to leave sinners in their sin	1. Because he cannot do anything else 2. Because that is what they deserve 3. Because heaven is not very big	☐
F. We should expect that many things about God will not be clear to us	1. Because of our limited human understanding 2. Because we have not heard enough sermons 3. Because we have not read the Bible enough	☐

Now send your answers to: ....

They will be marked and returned to you in due course

THE DOCTRINE OF GOD

SUBJECT: GOD CONTROLS EVERYTHING

COURSE 2
Lesson No. 9

COURSE NO. 2
Lesson No. 9

SUBJECT: GOD CONTROLS EVERYTHING

IN LESSON SEVEN we learned that

God is working-out a good plan and

IN LESSON EIGHT we learned that

though we may not fully understand God's plan, our duty is to live as God commands us in the scripture.

Providence
God's preservation of all things he has created and his government of all things according to his will and for his glory.

IN THIS LESSON we shall study the Bible evidence that God controls *everything.*

IF GOD DID NOT CONTROL EVERYTHING, HOW COULD HE BE SURE OF ANYTHING?

If even one thing was outside God's control, it could hinder what he wanted to do.

THE BIBLE DOES SHOW THAT GOD GOVERNS EVERYTHING.

There are SEVEN statements of scripture we shall look at now.

STATEMENT 1 God is in control of the universe and of all space.

Write out:

Isaiah 40:26

. . . .

. . . .

. . . .

. . . .

The total number of stars that might be seen with the naked eye if you travelled over the whole world is about 4,800. There are, however, many more stars than this; using telescopes and photography, astronomers estimate there are 100,000,000,000 stars in our galaxy and there are estimated to be 100,000,000 *other* galaxies, each with millions of their own stars! Professor Einstein estimated that total space is 100,000 times greater than what we can observe. SO WE SEE THE STRENGTH OF GOD'S POWER.

STATEMENT 2 God is in control of earth's weather

Write out:

Psalm 135:6, 7

. . . .

. . . .

. . . .

. . . .

. . . .

. . . .

. . . .

Read:

1. Matthew 16:2, 3
2. Jonah 1:4
3. Amos 4:7–9
4. Job 1:16, 19

Because God has created an orderly world, we can study its laws and learn to predict the weather.
Because he controls the things that cause the weather, God can use it for his purposes. It is not wrong, therefore, to pray about the weather. But it is wrong to grumble about it – to do so is to murmur against God.

We must accept the fact that God is also in control of natural calamities such as volcanoes, cyclones, droughts, etc. IT IS NOT THAT GOD ENJOYS SUCH THINGS BUT HE DOES HAVE HIS OWN GOOD REASONS FOR THEM. If we do not accept this, then the weather becomes one area where God is not in control and we have an immense problem – if God cannot control the weather, how can he be sure of working out his plan? Scripture insists God *does* control the weather. *We must accept what we may not understand.*

To think about:

". . . the winds and the seas, which are such impetuous and, one would think, even lawless creatures, they stir not, nor breathe, but to fulfil his word . . .'

God's Sovereignty by Elisha Coles, D.D. (1666)

STATEMENT 3 God is in control of the animal world

Write out:

Daniel 6:22
(first half only)

. . . .

. . . .

. . . .

Read:

1. Genesis 2:19
2. Exodus 8:6, 17, 24
3. Numbers 22:28
4. Jonah 1:17; 2:10
5. Matthew 10:29

The Bible has many examples of God controlling animals. The animals came to Noah's ark; the ravens fed Elijah; two bears were used to punish those who mocked Elisha.

It is not merely that God controls animals; scripture teaches that God actually cares for them. This fact is something that can encourage believers who are more valuable than animals. If God cares for the lesser, will he not certainly care for the greater?

QUAIL

STATEMENT 4 God is in control of human beings

Write out:

Psalm 139:16

. . . .

. . . .

. . . .

From this and other scriptures it is clear that God is concerned at all times with the details of peoples' lives. For example:

RAVEN

Write the correct Bible reference against each of these:

1.	BIRTH		I Samuel 16:1
2.	STATUS		Deuteronomy 8:18
3.	PROSPERITY		Proverbs 16:33
4.	SUCCESS OR FAILURE		Matthew 10:30
5.	SEEMINGLY ACCIDENTAL THINGS		Galatians 1:15–16
6.	SEEMINGLY SMALL THINGS		Luke 1:52

DESERT
SPARROW

Check, then proceed.

The correct references on page 3 are:

1. Galatians 1:15–16
2. I Samuel 16:1
3. Deuteronomy 8:18
4. Luke 1:52
5. Proverbs 16:33
6. Matthew 10:30

STATEMENT 5

God does not merely control good people, he also governs evil people so that they do not hinder the working of his plan. God works with evil people in two ways:

A. God sometimes stops people doing evil things.

Write out:

Genesis 20:6

. . . .

. . . .

. . . .

. . . .

God sometimes restrains people by directly affecting their experience. God sometimes restrains people by the normal laws of society or by the public example of good people.

Write out:

Romans 13:3

. . . .

. . . .

. . . .

B. God uses the evil things that people freely do for his good purposes.

Write out:

Acts 2:23

. . . .

. . . .

. . . .

Read:

Genesis 50:20

NOTE THIS: ☞ TO SAY THAT GOD CONTROLS EVIL PEOPLE does not mean that God is the cause of sin. People sin freely because they are already sinners. If God takes away his restraining influence, people plunge into the depths of sin.

Write out:

Romans 1:28

. . . .

. . . .

. . . .

NOTE THIS: ☞ THE FACT THAT GOD CONTROLS EVIL PEOPLE is a great source of assurance and joy to the believer. If this God is *our* God, then every situation into which we may come will be controlled by him for our good and his glory!

Write out:

Romans 8:28

. . . .

. . . .

. . . .

. . . .

STATEMENT 6 God does not only control individual people, he controls the affairs of whole nations.

Write out:

Psalm 22:28

. . . .

. . . .

. . . .

God's rule over all nations is well illustrated by the history of the Old Testament. For example:

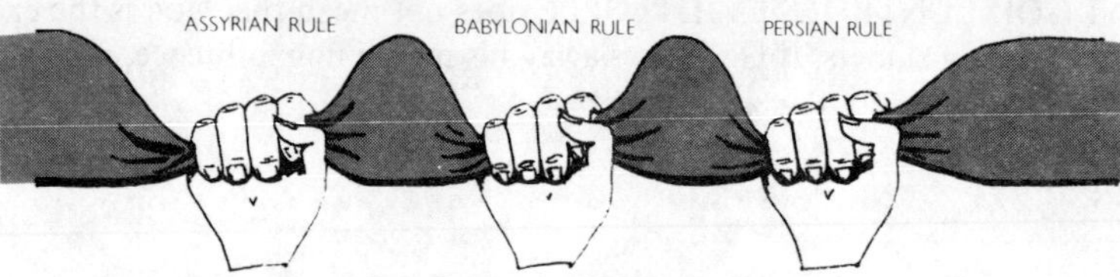

1. GOD USED
ASSYRIANS,
e.g. Isaiah 10:5–6

2. GOD USED
BABYLONIANS,
e.g. Jeremiah 25:9

3. GOD USED
PERSIANS,
e.g. Ezra 1:1–2

Write out the verses indicated:

Be glad that this same God is still in control of the nations TODAY!

Write out:

Ephesians 1:21

STATEMENT 7 God's people are always his special care

Write out:

I Timothy 4:10

. . . .

. . . .

. . . .

. . . .

To think about:

". . . He is a kind God, showering blessings upon all men (hence, he is their Preserver, Deliverer) but he is in a very special sense the Saviour of those who by faith embrace him . . . for to them he imparts everlasting life . . ."
Wm. Hendriksen, D.D.
Commentary on
I Timothy 4:10 (1957)

The word Saviour has a double meaning. It can be used to mean "a deliverer" – one who gives *physical* deliverance.
See: Judges 3:9; II Kings 13:5; Nehemiah 9:27.
By creating natural conditions in which all people can live and prosper, God is the Saviour, deliverer, of all physical life.

BUT FOR BELIEVERS God is especially a Saviour for he gives them eternal *spiritual* life.

Read:

Hebrews 11

There are many examples throughout Bible history showing *God's special care of his people.*

God's Plan –
see – lesson 7
page 6

It is not too much to say that God's Plan – to make sinners into saints from every nation – is *so* important to him that he arranges all the rest of human history to make sure this Plan is successful.

Write out:

I Corinthians 3:22, 23

. . . .

. . . .

. . . .

. . . .

WARNING!

Read:

Isaiah 5:11–13

To think about:

" . . . I can remember well the day and hour when I first received these truths (God's control of everything) in my own soul . . . and I can recollect how I felt I had grown on a sudden from a babe into a man . . . that I had made progress in scriptural knowledge, from having got a hold . . . of the clue to the truth of God . . ."
C. H. Spurgeon (1834–1892) *Metropolitan Tabernacle Pulpit,* Vol. 7, p. 85.

" . . . THOSE WHO REGARD NOT THE WORK OF THE LORD neither consider the operation of his hands . . . *are gone into captivity . . .*"

i.e. Because Israel *did not learn from Providence* what God was teaching them, they fell into unbelief and sin and had to be punished by being sent into captivity!

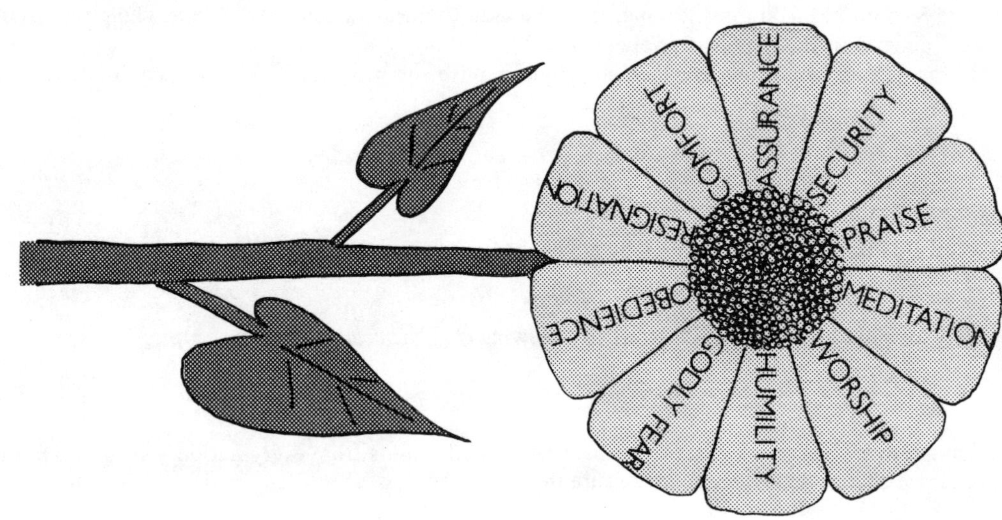

CONCLUSION:

If we really understand how wonderfully God works everything according to the purpose of his will, then we shall begin to experience a number of precious spiritual blessings. Surely to know a God so glorious, so successful, so careful, causes us to be filled with *humble, obedient, joyful worship.* We can be *assured* and *comforted* in all circumstances.

My name is .... My address is ....

QUESTIONS ABOUT LESSON 9

Only one answer is correct. Put here the number of the correct answer.

A. If God does not control everything

1. He can only be sure of some things
2. He can be sure of nothing
3. He can still be happy

☐

B. God created the world and now

1. Continues to govern it all
2. Leaves it to run itself
3. Keeps control of all religious things

☐

C. If we say God controls human beings

1. We make him responsible for their sins
2. Then they can never commit sins
3. We mean he uses the wicked actions they do of their own will for his purposes

☐

D. If God did not restrain people from wickedness

1. They would become unspeakably evil
2. It would make no difference
3. They would learn to control themselves

☐

E. God's *chief* purpose in all he does

1. Is to punish all who do evil
2. Is to make everyone obey him
3. Is to magnify his own glory by the salvation of believers

☐

F. Since God controls everything

1. It does not matter how we live
2. We should serve him in awe and joy
3. We can blame him for everything bad

☐

Now send your answers to: ....

They will be marked and returned to you in due course

THE DOCTRINE OF GOD

SUBJECT: THE LOVE OF GOD

COURSE 2
Lesson No. 10

SUBJECT: THE LOVE OF GOD

COURSE NO. 2
Lesson No. 10

1. INTRODUCTION

The Bible makes two important statements about the love of God.

Write out:

I John 4:8
(second part only)

A. . . . .

From this we learn that God's nature is love.

A man can cease to be loving, yet still be a man.
God cannot cease to be love without ceasing to be God, for love is his *essential nature.* Everything he does is done by *a loving nature*!

Write out:

Romans 5:8

B. . . . .

. . . .

. . . .

From this we learn that *God's love* is the thing most clearly shown by the death of Christ on the cross.

GOD'S LOVE THEREFORE IS A MOST IMPORTANT SUBJECT because

(i) HE HIMSELF IS LOVE and

(ii) CHRIST'S DEATH IS THE SUPREME PROOF OF GOD'S LOVE

If the Bible emphasises a subject so much as this, surely we ought also to study it very carefully. Among all the emotional feelings that God is said to have, love seems to take first place.

Write out:

I John 3:1
(first part only)

. . . .

. . . .

. . . .

2. THE NATURE OF GOD'S LOVE

When the New Testament was being written, the Greek language used by the people of that time had several words that mean "love". But the Holy Spirit guided the writers of the New Testament to use one word more than any other to describe *God's* love. Look carefully at this chart:

To think about:

"... The Greek and Roman world never dreamed of such love ... its gods were often lusting after women, but never loving sinners ... the New Testament writers had to introduce what was virtually a new word– agape – to express this love of God ..."
Dr. J. I. Packer (1973)
Knowing God, p. 137.

Greek word 'EROS'	Greek word 'STORGE'	Greek word 'PHILIA'	Greek word 'AGAPE'
sexual love	the love of a parent for offspring	love between friends – friendliness	the word used in the New Testament for *God's* love
Does not occur in the New Testament	Used twice in Greek New Testament – Romans 1:31 II Timothy 3:3	Noun and verb used 33 times in Greek New Testament See – James 4:4	Noun and verb forms occur more than 200 times

The first three kinds of love all come into existence because there is some reason for the attraction – attractive lover, devoted parent and child, kind friend.

THE SPECIAL FEATURE OF GOD'S LOVE IS THAT *HE CAN ALSO LOVE WHAT IS UNATTRACTIVE.*
GOD LOVED US WHILE WE WERE SINNERS.
GOD'S LOVE – AGAPE – IS AN UNUSUAL LOVE BECAUSE IT IS NOT LIMITED TO ATTRACTIVE THINGS.

Write out:

I John 4:19

....

....

....

The nature of God's love (contd.)

GOD'S LOVE appears in different ways according to the state of those to whom it is directed.

1.
Write out:

Ephesians 1:7

Special grace
see – page 4 of this lesson

Common grace
see – page 5 of this lesson

The love of God

special grace

common grace

MERCY

LONGSUFFERING

Those whom he will save from their sins by having Christ atone for their sins

2.
Write out:

Psalm 145:9

Those who are in any distress, whether believers or unbelievers

3.
Write out:

Romans 9:22

Those who are unbelieving and disobedient

3. THE OBJECTS OF GOD'S LOVE

A. GOD LOVES HIMSELF. Because he is pure and holy, it cannot be wrong for him to love himself.

Write out:

John 17:24
(last part only)

. . . .

. . . .

In the beginning before anything else existed God loved himself – i.e. there always was love between Father, Son and Spirit. We can best understand the statement "God is love" by remembering that there are three persons in God who can therefore love each other.

Read:

Romans 8:29

Special grace
God's gift of saving faith given to the elect only.

B. GOD LOVES HIS ELECT PEOPLE. Since believers are being conformed to the image of Christ and since God loves Christ, he must also love believers who are being made Christlike. Since God loves the Holy Spirit, he must also love believers who are showing the fruit of the Spirit in their lives. This love is sometimes called "Special grace". This love begins even before we are believers.

Noah .... GENESIS 6:8, 18

Write out:

John 14:21

. . . .

. . . .

. . . .

. . . .

. . . .

God loves his believing people:

Statement	Reference
(i) enough to prepare a kingdom for them	
(ii) in a special way, different from his love to others	
(iii) with a sacrificial love; he gave himself for them	
(iv) with a purpose, to make his children perfect	

Write the correct Bible reference against each of the statements

Ephesians 5:23 Ephesians 5:25

Hebrews 13:20–21 Matthew 25:34

Check, then proceed: The correct answers on page 4 are: (i) Matthew 25:34 (ii) Ephesians 5:23 (iii) Ephesians 5:25 (iv) Hebrews 13:20–21

C. GOD LOVES ALL THE CREATION. He made it all; it is natural that he should love what he has made even though angry that sin has spoiled it. Moreover, God must continue to sustain the world in order that his elect people should be able to live and come to salvation. God has lovingly promised to maintain his creation as long as need be. This is sometimes called "common grace".

Write out:

Genesis 8:22

. . . .

. . . .

. . . .

Common grace
God's gifts of temporal benefit freely enjoyed by all men.

D. GOD LOVES EVEN UNBELIEVING SINNERS. This love which is also "common grace" is shown in several ways. *It is not the same as his special love to his elect.* But it is a *real* love because:

(i) God gives unbelievers many physical and mental abilities, wealth and success which they do not deserve as sinners.

(ii) God waits patiently while unbelievers continually repeat their sinful acts. He does not destroy them at once as they deserve.

(iii) God commands that the good news of the gospel should be preached to all.

(iv) God now patiently offers to all people the resurrection of Christ as proof that the day of judgment will come – so he lovingly warns them though they neglect him.

(v) God has no pleasure in the death of the wicked.

(vi) God commands all to repent.

Write the correct Bible reference against each of these statements:

Luke 24:47	Matthew 5:45	Acts 17:30
I Peter 3:20	Acts 17:31	Ezekiel 18:23

Check, then proceed:

The correct answers on page 5 are: (i) Matthew 5:45 (ii) I Peter 3:20 (iii) Luke 24:47 (iv) Acts 17:31 (v) Ezekiel 18:23 (vi) Acts 17:30

---

4. PRACTICAL CONSEQUENCES OF GOD'S LOVE

A. IT GIVES THE BELIEVER COMFORT. God's love is eternal, unchanging, as is God himself.

Write out:

II Thessalonians 2:13

. . . .

. . . .

. . . .

. . . .

. . . .

To think about:

" . . . God's love is based on prior knowledge of the worst about me . . . no discovery now can disillusion him about me, in the way I am so often disillusioned about myself . . ."
Dr. J. I. Packer
Knowing God, 1973

The believer can know certainly that the gift of spiritual life and saving faith which he has received by God's gracious love is what God had always intended to give and so will never want to alter. This gives the believer a sense of security.

B. IT MAKES THE BELIEVER HOLY

Write out:

Romans 5:5

. . . .

. . . .

. . . .

. . . .

Since it is the *Holy* Spirit who causes us to feel God's love for us, having the knowledge of this love poured into us by such a one as he must make us holy. This knowledge must affect our whole way of living.

C. IT GIVES THE BELIEVER A MODEL TO FOLLOW

Write out:

Ephesians 4:32

. . . .

. . . .

Read:

Matthew 18:23–35

10,000 talents may be worth £10,000,000

100 pieces of silver may be worth £5

Jesus is teaching: God's love is shown to be in our hearts by our readiness to forgive those who have offended against us. Nothing anyone does to us can be worth more than £5 compared with the £10,000,000 we owe God – which he has forgiven us if we are believers, for Christ's sake!

SO IF WE CANNOT FORGIVE, THERE IS NO EVIDENCE WE HAVE EVER BEEN FORGIVEN!

D. IT GIVES THE BELIEVER GROUNDS TO PRESENT THE GOSPEL *PERSUASIVELY*

Write out:

Romans 2:4

. . . .

. . . .

. . . .

. . . .

THE BELIEVER CAN USE ALL THESE REASONS ARISING FROM GOD'S LOVE TO PLEAD WITH PEOPLE. IT CAN NEVER BE SAID THAT GOD IS INDIFFERENT TO THE PLIGHT OF UNBELIEVERS.

(i) Since God freely gives so many blessings even to unbelievers, *ought* they not to worship him?

(ii) Since God so patiently waits while unbelievers neglect him and judgment delays, *ought* they not to repent and seek forgiveness?

(iii) Since God commands that all nations be told of the gospel, are not unbelievers without excuse?

(iv) Since God gave his only Son to die for sinners, how can any sinner be indifferent?

E. IT GIVES THE BELIEVER THE CONTENT OF HIS MESSAGE. The Christian preacher can declare and explain from the scriptures:

(i) How Christ's work in his life, death and resurrection is the *expression of God's love* and is sufficient for anyone's spiritual needs.

(ii) How repentance and faith are the *chief gifts of God's love* to all his children.

(iii) How everyone who comes to Christ in repentance and faith sincerely seeking salvation will be *welcomed by God.*

(iv) How wilful *neglect of God's love* is a sign of spiritual death in a person and is certain to end in their everlasting punishment.

Write out:

(i) I John 4:9

. . . .

(ii) Acts 11:18

. . . .

(iii) Romans 10:13

. . . .

(iv) Hebrews 2:3 (first part only)

. . . .

My name is .... My address is ....

QUESTIONS ABOUT LESSON 10

Only one answer is correct. Put here the number of the correct answer.

A. We ought to think carefully about God's love	1. Because it is his nature 2. Because it is a nice subject 3. Because everyone understands it	☐
B. God's love is of a kind that is	1. The same as human love 2. Different from human love 3. Unknowable	☐
C. The scripture teaches us that	1. God loves everyone the same 2. God only loves Christians 3. Believers are objects of God's special love	☐
D. We know that there is a love of God to all the world	1. Because it is only reasonable that there should be 2. Because of his longsuffering patience and his good gifts to all people 3. Because the world needs it	☐
E. Personal knowledge of the love of God	1. Is something we learn by reasoning 2. Is discovered by reading the Bible 3. Is an experience the Holy Spirit gives us which affects our whole lives	☐
F. God has a special love for his elect, therefore	1. We should not preach to all people but only to the elect 2. There is nothing we can say to non-Christians 3. We should preach to all people because God has told us to do so	☐

Now send your answers to: ....

They will be marked and returned to you in due course

THE DOCTRINE OF GOD
SUBJECT: GOD IS A TRINITY

COURSE 2
Lesson No. 11

SUBJECT: GOD IS A TRINITY

COURSE NO. 2
Lesson No. 11

IN OUR LAST LESSON we learned

that God's essential nature is love. He cannot cease to be love without ceasing to be God and

that God can be love because he is three persons – Father, Son and Spirit. Because God is a Trinity love can flow between the three divine persons, each to the other; so God can be love in himself.

IN THIS LESSON we shall study

what it means to say God is a Tri-unity.

NOTE THIS:

This teaching is revealed only in the Christian scriptures. NO OTHER RELIGION HAS SUCH A GOD. The Christian God is *unique*. We shall never therefore be able *to understand* his nature, though we shall be able to state what it is from scripture.

Write out:

II Corinthians 13:14

. . . .

. . . .

. . . .

. . . .

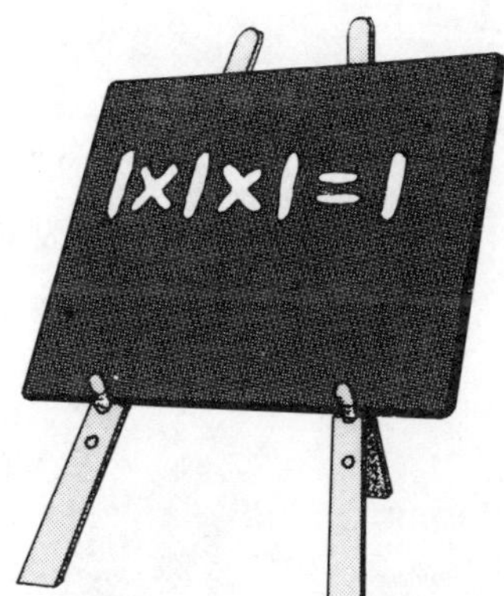

Page 8 of this lesson studies this uniqueness in detail.

THE TRINITY IS UNIQUE. We know of nothing else which can be three things and yet each of the three be the whole at the same time as being three. *Illustrations must* all fall short of this unique kind of Being.

1. THAT GOD IS A TRINITY IS MOST SATISFYING TO HUMAN EXPERIENCE

Moloch - a Baal of Canaan

A. People have an inbuilt consciousness that there is a greater power than they – a God *"above them"*, unseen but sensed.

B. People feel a need to be able *to see* this God and handle him.

C. People feel a need to have *the presence* of God with them when facing the various circumstances of life.

Unbelievers try to meet these three needs themselves by:

A. Worshipping nature, the forces of the universe; these are powers greater than human power and do *create "awe"*.

B. Worshipping images, icons and idols, or systems of philosophy; these are all attempts to make God *visible*.

C. Worshipping demons, spirits; using magic ceremonies, drugs; these all give an idea of a *mysterious presence*.

For the Christian, the Trinity satisfies these three needs because:

A. God the Father is the unseen, supreme source of all things; God *above us*.

B. God the Son is God incarnate, visible, tangible; God *with us*.

C. God the Spirit is God *in us*, causing our spirits to know the things of God.

Babylonian replica sheeps liver used in fortune telling

Write out:

Ephesians 4:6

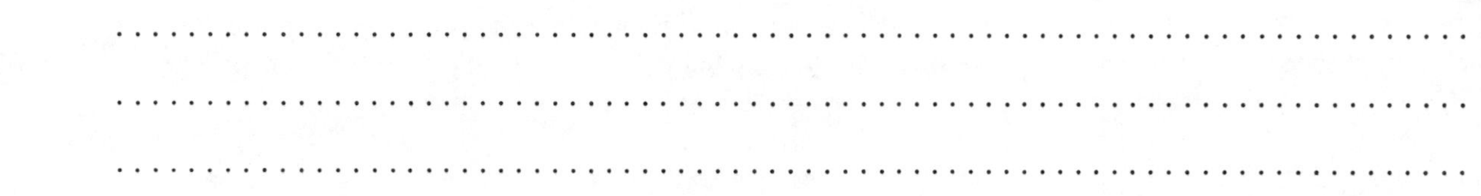

2. **THE TRUTH OF THE TRINITY COMES TO LIGHT THROUGH THE PROGRESSIVE REVELATION OF SCRIPTURE**

Write out:

I Peter 1:2

. . . .

. . . .

. . . .

Here Peter makes a clear statement of the Tri-unity of God. But *before he met Jesus* Peter was an orthodox Jew who would have known only of the unity of God. All Jews had to recite twice daily:

Write out:

Deuteronomy 6:4

. . . .

. . . .

When Peter met Jesus and lived with him for a while, he was compelled to admit that Jesus was God.

To think about:

To be a son is to have the same nature as the father.

Write out:

Matthew 16:16

. . . .

. . . .

. . . .

On the day of Pentecost Peter experienced the miracle of being filled by the Holy Spirit; what he experienced then was God filling him.

Write out:

Acts 2:33

. . . .

. . . .

. . . .

. . . .

And so in the progressive experience of the early church the doctrine of the Trinity has become an exciting reality! Peter has met the three Persons of the one God!

3. THE OLD TESTAMENT SUGGESTS THE DOCTRINE OF THE TRINITY

Monotheism
the teaching that there is only one God. Since there is only *one* God, the Trinity cannot be a doctrine of three gods, i.e. Tritheism.

Contrary to the beliefs of other nations, the Jews always held to the truth of monotheism. Other nations worshipped many gods. But at the same time there are many evidences in the Old Testament scriptures that this "oneness" is not an *indivisible* oneness. Even a statement like Deuteronomy 6:4 means not so much "God is a unity" as "God is unique; there is no other God".

A. There are a number of passages where God speaks of himself as plural: "us".

Write out:

Genesis 1:26
(first part only)

. . . .

. . . .

See also:

Genesis 3:22; 11:7

Read:

Genesis 16:7–13
Judges 13:1–22

B. There are passages where "the Angel of the Lord" is spoken of as God though distinguished from God. This illustrates the idea of plurality in God.

Write out:

Genesis 16:14

. . . .

. . . .

. . . .

. . . .

C. There are passages where God to deliver his people promises to raise up a king who is also called God. This illustrates the idea of plurality in God.

Write out:

Jeremiah 23:5
(last part only)

. . . .

. . . .

Jeremiah 23:6
(last part only)

. . . .

. . . .

D. There are passages where God is addressed in a three-fold way.

Write out:

Isaiah 6:3

Read:

Numbers 6:24–26

4. THE NEW TESTAMENT ASSUMES THE DOCTRINE OF THE TRINITY

To think about:

" . . . Seven Spirits (Rev. 5:6) . . . it seems most probable that we should think of the number 7 as signifying perfection . . . the whole expression pointing to the Holy Spirit. The number 7 may be derived from Isaiah 11:2 . . . the 7 modes of operation of the Spirit . . ."
Leon Morris, M.Th. (1969). *Commentary on Revelation.*

The reason why the New Testament can be so much clearer than the Old is because in New Testament times both God the Son and God the Spirit had been *clearly* revealed. *Now* the Triune God is *a fact of experience.*

There are certain qualities used to describe God (the Father). These are also used to describe God (the Son) and God (the Spirit), as follows:

GOD THE SON		*GOD THE SPIRIT*
1. John 1:3	Omnipotence	1. I Corinthians 12:11
2. John 13:3	Omniscience	2. I Corinthians 2:10, 11
3. Matthew 28:20	Omnipresence	3. Revelation 5:6

omniscient * omnipotent * omnipresent *
SON
GOD
FATHER * SPIRIT

Since the Son and the Spirit both equally possess the same attributes as God the Father, it is clear *God is Triune.* It is *this Triune God* that the disciples are commanded to preach.

Write out:

Matthew 28:19

5. THE NEW TESTAMENT MAKES PLAIN STATEMENTS OF THE DOCTRINE OF THE TRINITY

A. Jesus Christ is plainly called God:

Write out:

Romans 9:5

. . . .

. . . .

. . . .

The Holy Spirit is plainly called God:

Write out:

II Corinthians 3:17

. . . .

. . . .

The Father is plainly called God:

Write out:

I Corinthians 8:6
(first part only)

. . . .

. . . .

. . . .

There is no other God spoken of in the New Testament.

Look up these verses and write the correct word against each of the statements:

B.

Statement		
In John 3:8 the believer is said – to be born of the . . .		1.
In John 5:21 the believer is said – to be quickened by the . . .		2.
In John 1:13 the believer is said – to be born of . . .		3.

Write out:

Romans 11:36

. . . .

. . . .

. . . .

Check, then proceed: The correct answers on page 6 are: 1. SPIRIT 2. SON 3. GOD

Read:

Ephesians 1:3–14

Then fill in the correct verse numbers where this phrase occurs:

To think about:

"... It is not in a text here and there that the New Testament testifies to the doctrine of the Trinity. The whole book is Trinitarian to the core; all its teaching is built on the assumption of the Trinity; and its allusions to the Trinity are frequent, easy and confident ..."

ALSO:

"... As we read, we are kept in continual contact with three persons who act each as a distinct Person, and yet who are in a deep sense, one ..."
from *Biblical Doctrine of Trinity* by Prof. B. B. Warfield (1851–1921)

C. The apostles freely use the fact of God as a Trinity in their writings, e.g.:

The work of *the Father*	The work of *the Son*	The work of *the Spirit*
ELECTION PREDESTINATION	REDEMPTION FORGIVENESS	BELIEF SEALING
v. 3 to v ...	v. 7 to v ...	v. 13 to v ...

"To the praise of his glory" 1. v ... 2. v ... 3. v ...

The phrase "to the praise of his glory" divides these verses into three sections. The same pattern – of three persons acting in unity as one God – in our salvation is also seen in passages like:

II Thessalonians 2:13–14 Titus 3:4–6 and I Peter 1:2

D. Jesus in his teaching speaks clearly of three equal persons in the one God, e.g.:

Write out: ....

John 15:26 ....

....

....

....

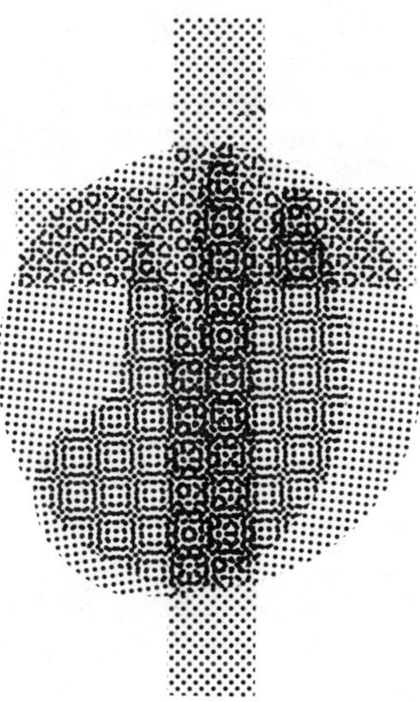

This verse teaches:

The Spirit, Jesus and the Father are three distinct persons.

All three are completely united in the same act of salvation.

All three live in one eternal fellowship.

6. WRONG IDEAS ABOUT THE TRINITY

To think about:

" . . . The man who will get nearest to understanding the Trinity as the New Testament understands it, is not the philosopher, or the historian, but the man who knows for himself the God who made him, who has redeemed him, and whose power is undeniably producing in his life the fruit of holiness . . ."
from *The Living God*
by R. T. France (1970, IVP)

Because the nature of God's Trinitarian existence is so different from anything we can experience, it is easy to make mistakes in our thinking about it. E.g:

Some have denied that God is three distinct persons. They suggest God can appear either as Father, or as Son, or as Spirit. When he is one of these, the others do not exist.

Others have suggested that Jesus and the Spirit are different persons from the Father and that they two are not divine but only creatures of lower rank.

Others have suggested the Spirit is not a person but only divine power in action.

THE SCRIPTURE VERSES WE HAVE ALREADY STUDIED SHOW THAT THE SUGGESTIONS ABOVE ARE WRONG.

Biblical "Tri-unity" means:

A. Perfect threeness	=	there can only be the three no one of the three can ever be either of the others
B. Perfect oneness	=	each of the three persons is the whole God no one of the persons acts without the others
C. Perfect orderliness	=	the Father is always the unseen source the Son is always the visible expression the Spirit is also unseen, always bringing the divine purposes to perfection

N.B. This orderliness *cannot* mean that one person is more important than any other because each is the whole God. Never emphasise one person as more important than the others.

ANY TEACHING ABOUT THE TRINITY WHICH DENIES ANY OF THESE THREE POINTS IS CONTRADICTING WHAT THE SCRIPTURES TEACH AND MUST BE WRONG.

7. THE PRACTICAL VALUES OF THE DOCTRINE OF THE TRINITY

All Bible doctrines have practical consequences. What we believe must always affect how we behave. That is true of *this* doctrine also.

A. An important part of the attitude of worship is a sense of awe in the presence of mystery. Tri-unity is a mystery to us. This unique mode of existence is far superior to anything we humans know. It is excellent, glorious, worthy of worship.

See this lesson, page 2.

B. As we have already seen, a Triune God meets the three needs of the human heart. Such a God is above us, with us and in us.

To think about:

"... the doctrine of the Trinity is the foundation of all our communion with God and comfortable dependence upon him ..."
Baptist Confession of Faith, London, England, 1689.

C. The Tri-unity of God gives him a unique beauty. The miracle of "threeness-which-is-also-oneness" means such a perfection of harmony of understanding, of abilities, of purpose, as is beyond our human experience. There are no secrets within God, no breakdowns in communication.

D. The three persons unite in assisting our worship. We worship the Father by means of the Spirit's power because the Son has made a way.

NO WONDER PAUL EXCLAIMS:

Write out:

Romans 11:33

....

....

....

....

NOTE THIS:  CAREFUL THOUGHT ABOUT THE TRINITY WILL ENRICH OUR WORSHIP

NOTE THIS:  God's work in the hearts of sinners making them believers is a work of the Trinity.

(i) a. The Father planned it all

b. The Father sent the Son

c. The Son came, lived, died, rose again and now intercedes for all for whom he died

d. The Spirit searches out, convicts and convinces all for whom Christ died, bringing them to belief and repentance.

Write the correct Bible reference against each of the statements:

Ephesians 1:4 Hebrews 10:19, 20

John 3:16 John 16:7–15

(ii) If we are conscious of sorrow for sin and drawn to belief in Jesus, that is the Spirit's work. Since the three persons are united we know that if the Spirit works in people, then Christ also died for them and God the Father also chose them. To doubt this is to suggest the three persons in God are not united in purpose!

(iii) The Father accepted the offering of the Son and raised him from the dead. That means that all whom Christ represented must be saved by the Spirit and brought to heaven. Not one *can* be lost or there would be a break down between the work of the three persons! God cannot lose any for whom Christ died!

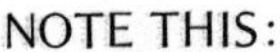

NOTE THIS:  CAREFUL THOUGHT ABOUT THE TRINITY WILL GIVE THE BELIEVER ASSURANCE, COMFORT AND HOPE.

Check, then proceed: The correct answers on page 10 are: a. Ephesians 1:4 b. John 3:16 c. Hebrews 10:19, 20 d. John 16:7–15

Sanctification
To separate for a holy use.

The sanctification of the believer is a work of the Trinity.

(i) a. God desires holiness

b. The Son died that we might be purified

c. The Spirit creates holiness in us

Write the correct Bible reference against each of the statements

I Thessalonians 4:3 II Thessalonians 2:13 Hebrews 9:14

(ii) Because all three persons are concerned to make believers holy, no people can claim to be chosen by God unless the Spirit actually produces holiness in their lives. The Spirit must actually sanctify all whom God chose, or there is a breakdown in the work of the Trinity.

(iii) Holiness can only come to us through Christ's work on the cross, since that is the method the Father planned to use to save sinners. We cannot be made holy by visiting any special place, doing any special action, or having a special ceremony done to us. Holiness comes only by obedience to Christ. To deny this is to suggest the Trinity is not satisfied with the work of one of the Persons.

NOTE THIS:

CAREFUL THOUGHT ABOUT THE TRINITY WILL HELP US TO EXAMINE OUR SPIRITUAL EXPERIENCE AND ENSURE WE ARE NOT DECEIVED

Check, then proceed: The correct answers on page 11 are:

a. I Thessalonians 4:3
b. Hebrews 9:14
c. II Thessalonians 2:13

It should be clear by now that the doctrine of the Trinity has a practical effect in all parts of Christian life and service.

We conclude this study with a long quotation from a book about the Trinity.

> "There is a God who is angry with us because of our sins. He sent God the Son, conceived by the Holy Spirit, sinlessly to assume human nature, and to keep fully his law on our behalf. Christ, the guiltless, died as our substitute, bearing the condemnation which our sins deserve, and which God's justice demands. The Holy Spirit brings us to grieve for our sins, and to turn from them. He brings us to rest on what Christ has done for sinners. He brings us into union with Christ, so that his perfect character is reckoned to our account, and our sins are accepted as having been punished when Christ died. God the Father now receives us as his sons and becomes a Father to us. The Lord Jesus Christ stands to us as an elder brother in God's family. The Holy Spirit is within us, and inwardly assures us that we are the children of God. Each Person of the Trinity is involved. IT MUST BE PLAIN THAT WITHOUT THE DOCTRINE OF THE TRINITY THE WHOLE PLAN OF REDEMPTION FALLS TO PIECES."

From the book *The Three are One*, by Stuart Olyott, E. P. (1979)

Write out: . . . .

Ephesians 2:18 . . . .

My name is .... My address is ....

Only one answer is correct.
Put here the number of the correct answer.

QUESTIONS ABOUT LESSON 11

A. It is not easy for us to study the doctrine of the Trinity because
1. It is only an old Jewish idea
2. It is something clever Greek philosophers thought of
3. It is unlike any mode of Being that we know of

☐

B. It is good to study the doctrine of the Trinity because
1. People will think us clever
2. It will help us understand all other Bible truths better
3. We cannot be Christians at all unless we do

☐

C. There are no clear statements of the doctrine of the Trinity in the Old Testament because
1. The three persons of God had not then been revealed
2. The Jews had not invented it
3. The Jews could not have understood it

☐

D. In the New Testament the doctrine of the Trinity is
1. Suggested, if you look hard for it
2. Clearly stated and everywhere assumed
3. Only taught by Paul

☐

E. If we go wrong in our thinking about the Trinity
1. It does not really matter very much
2. We shall soon be wrong about other Bible truths
3. It proves we are not clever people

☐

F. The doctrine of the Trinity has a practical value
1. On Trinity Sunday, once a year
2. So that hymns can have three verses
3. In deepening the meaning of all the activities of the believer's life

☐

Now send your answers to: ....

They will be marked and returned to you in due course.

LIST OF SCRIPTURE REFERENCES

KEY TO QUESTION PAGES

LIST OF SCRIPTURE REFERENCES USED IN THIS STUDY COURSE

KEY TO QUESTION PAGES OF COURSE NO. 2

Lesson 1	Lesson 2	Lesson 3	Lesson 4	Lesson 5
A 1	A 1	A 2	A 1	A 2
B 2	B 3	B 3	B 2	B 1
C 1	C 2	C 1	C 3	C 2
D 3	D 2	D 2	D 2	D 1
E 1	E 3	E 3	E 1	E 2
F 3	F 2	F 2	F 1	F 1

Lesson 6	Lesson 7	Lesson 8	Lesson 9	Lesson 10	Lesson 11
A 2	A 2	A 2	A 2	A 1	A 3
B 3	B 3	B 1	B 1	B 2	B 2
C 1	C 3	C 2	C 3	C 3	C 1
D 2	D 1	D 1	D 1	D 2	D 2
E 3	E 1	E 2	E 3	E 3	E 2
F 1	F 3	F 1	F 2	F 3	F 3

NOTES

NOTES

NOTES